Jewish Bridges

Russian Jews Arriving for Leipzig Messe, 1834. Watercolor by Georg Emanuel Opiz. Courtesy of Leipziger Messeamt.

JEWISH BRIDGES

East to West

Michael Cohn

PRAEGER

**Westport, Connecticut
London**

Library of Congress Cataloging-in-Publication Data

Cohn, Michael.
      Jewish bridges : East to West / Michael Cohn.
          p.   cm.
      Includes bibliographical references and index.
      ISBN 0–275–95463–3 (alk. paper)
      1. Jews—Europe, Eastern—Migrations. 2. Jews, Eastern European—
Europe, Western—Economic conditions. 3. Jews, Eastern European—
United States—Economic conditions. 4. Jewish businessmen.
5. Jewish entertainers—United States. 6. Jews in the motion
picture industry—United States. I. Title.
DS135.E8C64   1996
305.892′4047—dc20   96–15386

British Library Cataloguing in Publication Data is available.

Library of Congress Catalog Card Number: 96–15386
ISBN: 0–275–95463–3

First published in 1996

Praeger Publishers, 88 Post Road West, Westport, CT 06881
An imprint of Greenwood Publishing Group, Inc.

Printed in the United States of America

The paper used in this book complies with the
Permanent Paper Standard issued by the National
Information Standards Organization (Z39.48–1984).

10 9 8 7 6 5 4 3 2 1

To our parents
Siegmund and Lucie Cohn (nee Wiener)
Walton and Augusta Strauss (nee Rosenthal)
who were a blend of East and West

Contents

Photo essay to follow chapter 4.

Preface

This is a book of Jewish cultural migration, about a process of cultural adaptions by those Jews not allowed to assimilate and, at times, the geographical transference of Eastern Jewish settlements to the West with as little change as possible.

This history is of importance because it is part of an ongoing process. Today the overwhelming majority of the 120,000 Jews in Germany formerly lived in what was the Soviet Union. There are large groups of recently arrived Russian Jews living in New York and London. These immigrants, like their predecessors, are influenced by and are also an influence on their new countries of residence.

There never were any physical obstacles to travelling on the great plain that stretches from the Ural Mountains to the North Sea. There are neither mountains nor deserts, only some wide rivers to cross— and these serve as much as highways of transportation as obstacles to travel. National borders and their guards are no barrier, for the guards can be evaded or bribed, something that has happened to border guards of all nationalities and times of history. It is not surprising that Jews, as well as other groups, travelled across this plain. Sometimes the Jews travelled in small caravans of traders, at other times as massive waves of immigrants several million strong.

From 1648 to 1933, the advantages of living were all in the West, and the Jews followed the available advantages. From 1933 to 1945, all movement was a flight from Hitler's legions, who were planning the extermination of all Jews. From 1945 on the westward flow began again. First there was a trickle, then a stream, and finally a flood of people. Israel attracted some of the immigrants, but Israel was too small to afford scope to so many. For thousands of Russian Jews, Europe and America were more attractive.

The Jews who came from the East did not come without gifts to the West. They brought their culture, their folktales, and the language of Yiddish. They brought their political skills, sharpened in the ghettos, and their flexibility in trading, and they applied these to the economies and politics of the West, giving many industries and ideas an Eastern Jewish flavor.

Those Jews who were already living in the West and, to a certain extent, had adjusted themselves to the culture of their non-Jewish neighbors tried to set themselves apart from the floods of Jewish newcomers. Almost always this "setting apart" was cultural rather than biological. It was seldom successful for long. As the newcomers learned to adjust themselves to the new setting of the cultures of the West, they became more and more acceptable to the Western Jews. It could not be any other way, since the numbers of Eastern Jewish immigrants exceeded the number of Jews living in the Western countries.

Terms in three languages, Yiddish, German, and Hebrew, are used in this book. A definition follows each term the first time it is used. There is also a glossary at the end of the book for the convenience of the reader. However, this confusion of tongues is compounded when it comes to place names. When the name of the city is only slightly altered, as is the case of Warsaw, for instance, I have used the conventional English spelling. In other cases I have placed the alternative names of the towns in parentheses to avoid confusion. The shifting of national boundaries and the Russian habit of changing the name of a city each time the political situation changes makes Eastern European geography difficult. As a result, for instance, St. Petersburg becomes Petrograd, then Leningrad, and at present is St. Petersburg again.

My knowledge of Yiddish and Hebrew is faulty, at best, so I have tried to follow what seems to be standard practice, but experts in these languages may find faults in spelling or precise definitions.

The days when social scientists considered themselves to be culturally and politically neutral are long over. It is therefore important that the reader know something about the author and his background. I was born in Leipzig in 1924, moved to Berlin at the age of three, and to New York at the age of nine. My father's family can be traced to Danzig in 1840; later they moved to Berlin, but my father spent part of his youth in Budapest. His mother's family came to Berlin from what was, most of the time, northern Poland.

My mother's father came from Bohemia, her mother from Leipzig. This mixture seems to make me a fairly typical "German Jew."

Politically my father was a Marxist, but he left the Communist party in disgust in 1932. My mother was active in the Zionist movement in her youth, as was her father.

I consider myself an American Jew. I have visited Germany frequently since my emigration. In 1946 it was courtesy of the U.S. Army; in 1951 and 1971, I was in transit elsewhere. Since 1985 my wife and I have been in Germany almost annually for research and lectures. I am a professional anthropologist with a number of works on Jewish subjects to my credit. In 1987 I coauthored *From Germany to Washington Heights*, and authored in 1989, *Medieval Justice: The Trial of the Jews of Trent*. The latter was a catalogue for an exhibition that I guest curated, and I also created an exhibit on the Soviet Jewish settlement of Birobidjian in 1993. In 1994 my *Jews in Germany: 1945–1993* was published.

For twenty-five years I was senior instructor in history and anthropology at the Brooklyn Children's Museum in Crown Heights, near the headquarters of the Lubavitcher Hasidim. At present I am adjunct anthropologist at the Yeshiva University Museum.

This book is a report of an ongoing research project and therefore must be considered incomplete. The culture of the Jews is in constant flux, and Jewish groups as well as individuals are in constant movement. It is hoped that this work will stimulate the interest of Jewish and non-Jewish observers as well as my fellow professionals.

Acknowledgments

"No man is an Island," wrote John Donne, the English poet. Neither is any author working alone. I have received generous help and information from many, only some of whom are listed here by name.

Among the libraries, the archives of the Leo Baeck Institute must be mentioned, where Dr. Diane R. Spielmann dug out so much material for my use. The archivists of the YIVO Institute for Jewish Research found not only much written but also much pictorial information. The Karl Marx Memorial Library in London was helpful, not only searching their own shelves but referring me to other sources in London for additional data.

Sylvia Herskowitz, Director of the Yeshiva University Museum, gave me her full support and her help from her wide knowledge of Jewish culture. Rabbi Herschel Gluck of the *Chabad Lubevitch* in London was an unfailing counselor. Aaron Adlerstein, long a leader of the Jewish congregation in Leipzig, gave of his time and knowledge, as did Dr. Irene Runge of the Berlin *Jüdischer Kulturverein*.

Dr. Klaus Herrmann of Concordia University in Montreal was as helpful as always.

Barbara John, who bears the long German title of *Ausland-beauftragte des Senats von Berlin*, gave us time from her hectic schedule of caring for the new immigrants to Germany's capital to share with us her warm, human approach to the history and problems of the immigrants from the East. To her and all our special helpers in Europe, thanks are due.

Knowledge and assistance to the author also came from friends and relatives, who rummaged in their memories and their closets for documents, pictures, and information relating to the Jewish bridges from East to West. I received special help from my brother, Peter J. Cohn, my cousins Edgar J. Malecki, Joan and Charles Merber, and Paul L. Wiener, as well as from my brother-in-law Dr. John Strauss. Leonard Cohan aided with both advice and memories. The pictures they found were supplemented by their own information and by what they remembered from all they had been told by deceased relatives about the fur trade, the textile trade, and the history of Jewish life.

The staff of the German Information Service in New York and their counterparts in the Inter Nationes in Germany helped tremendously in arranging appointments with informants and with travel in the German Bundesrepublik.

The workers of Modernage Photographic Service made miracles happen in resurrecting faded snapshots for the illustrations in this book. The editorial crew of Praeger Publishers was unfailingly helpful in keeping this work on track despite medical emergencies and howling snowstorms.

It is difficult to thank my wife, Susan S. Cohn, adequately. She functioned as picture editor, fellow researcher, English editor, and sounding board during the long period of this book's creation at the same time that she put up with my lack of attention to household chores. She shares with me the credit for this work.

For any and all faults of omission and commission in this book, however, I bear full responsibility.

1

The Eastern Setting

A major migration of Jews from Germany and Austria into Eastern Europe[1] started in the fourteenth century. To get Jews to move into his kingdom, Casimir the Great of Lithuania offered them a charter that defined their rights and privileges in 1357.[2] His efforts were expanded to the newly united kingdom of Lithuania and Poland by Casimir IV, who came to the throne in 1445.

The charters that the kings of the Jagellon dynasty offered placed the Jews directly under the king as an autonomous group free of the jurisdiction of feudal lords, bishops, or municipal councils. They would be free to administer their own communities and their own markets. Justice would be administered by officials of the king under Magdeburg Law, a set of rules first developed in the German city of Magdeburg on the Elbe and later adopted as a basic constitution by most of the cities of Poland.[3] Magdeburg Law was a typical medieval charter. A somewhat similar set of regulations, Lübeck Laws, governed the German traders of the Hansaic League wherever they lived, in England, Norway, Germany, or Russia.

Italian merchants had extracted a similar autonomous status from the Empire of Byzantium (Istanbul) and from the rulers of the Crusader states in the Holy Land. The charters of the Hansaic merchants and Italian traders are no longer used, but the charters granted to the Jews of Poland and Lithuania set a pattern that still has influence on the Jewish communities of Europe today.

The Jews examined the offered charters, listened to the inducements of the Polish kings, and many of them moved east. They brought their craft skills and their trading connections with them. They also brought their language, a Middle German dialect interlaced with Hebrew loan words that later would become Yiddish.

As an autonomous group, the Jews were free to worship as they pleased, elect their own administration and determine their rules of membership, that is, rules to decide who is a Jew. Relations between Jew and Jew were to be governed by a Jewish court, the *Bet Din*. The community formed a *kahilla*, a term that is still in use today. By 1551 the kahilla of the city of Vilna (Lithuania) was given full judicial authority.[4] Disputes between Jews and Christians were to be tried before the representative of the king, not in municipal court, where the Christians had more influence. All of these complicated relationships were spelled out in the charters and did not depend on the goodwill or daily mood of the king. Like all medieval charters, all laws expired at the death of the king and had to be reconfirmed by the new king at his accession, and naturally gifts were required to prevent the new king from changing the charters.

For the Jews this arrangement was much preferable to the conditions they faced in the Habsburg dominions and the German states. In those jurisdictions Jews were subject to many special taxes. They were forced to wear "Jew hats" on the streets. If they appeared in court, they were forced to stand on pigs' skins and subjected to all kinds of insulting oaths. Rising religious fanaticism among the Christians in this period also had resulted in the expulsion of all Jews from many towns, often connected with false charges of ritual child murder or desecration of the Host.[5]

The move to the kingdom of Poland made economic sense to the Jews. The militant Ottoman Turks were advancing up the Danube and in the Mediterranean Sea, closing the old trade routes as they came. The city of Byzantium was stormed by the Turks in 1453, thus ending the existence of the Roman Empire, which had endured as a major trading power for 2,000 years. The first Turkish siege of Vienna in 1529 was unsuccessful, but the Turks already had subjugated or destroyed the armed forces of the Serbs, Wallachians, and the Hungarians. Turkish sultans controlled the entire Near East to Persia, all of North Africa, and Greece. Their galleys raided southern Italy and Spain. The Khans of the Crimea paid them tribute. A tribute of boys was laid on all Christians in their dominions, boys who would make up the feared Turkish janizaries, or infantry. Access to the trade of the Orient now went through the steppes of Poland and the Ukraine to the Caspian Sea and Persia. Fine furs, silks and other fine textiles, gems, spices, and timber travelled up the rivers through Polish territory to the Baltic and from there to Western Europe. In return Europe exported woolens, iron, silver, and, later, guns and gunpowder. Russia and Poland also exported furs, walrus and mammoth ivory, and amber.

The coming of the Jews was of tremendous advantage to the Polish kings. As an autonomous group, they would be loyal to the kings rather than to the feudal lords. The large sums they paid as taxes would go directly into the royal treasury. To this would be added the more or less voluntary gifts given to the kings when a charter was to be renewed or a court case decided. Because the Jews had no local loyalties, the kings used them as treasurers, tax farmers, and custom duty collectors. The nobles, busy with feudal warfare, followed the king's example. They hired Jews to manage their estates, run their mills and distilleries, and act as innkeepers. This system resulted in a maximum cash benefit to the king and the nobles and a commission to the Jewish managers. It also deflected the hatred of the Christian population from their feudal oppressors to the Jews, who were their visible exploiters as tax collectors and estate managers.

The Polish kingdom of this period covered an enormous territory. The armies of the Polish kings had smashed the crusading order of Teutonic knights at Tannenberg in 1410 and eventually made them feudal subjects of Poland. The Baltic coast was under Polish control. The Ukraine, Byelarus, Poland itself, and Russia east to Smolensk were subject to the kings of the Jagellon dynasty.

However, this empire was surrounded by enemies. Russia was always hostile to Poland for religious as well as political reasons. Poland was primarily Roman Catholic, and Russia gave its allegiance to the Greek Orthodox Church of Byzantium. The Swedes wanted control of both sides of the Baltic. The Turks and the Crimean Tartars had no love for the Poles. Until 1648 the Habsburgs, although hostile, were no threat. Their lands were disrupted by the Thirty Years' War, which had broken out between Catholic and Protestant German states and ended by wiping out half or more of the population of Bohemia and Germany.

In this situation, surrounded by enemies without and threatened by feudal discord within, the kings of Poland were only too glad to foster Jewish communities and to assign them streets and sections of towns to control.

Within the Jewish communities, as in most medieval trading communities, power fell into the hands of the wealthier merchants, who controlled the purse. The *parnassim*, the elected leaders of the kahilla, were always drawn from the Jewish upper classes. Competition to belong to the *Roshe Ha Kalal*, the heads of the community, was fierce. This was because the offices gave social prestige and also economic advantage, through having a voice in the affairs of the Jewish courts and the markets. Members of the governing board of the Jewish community of Vilna had to be of good reputation, be married for six to ten years, and give special contributions to the kahilla and its charitable institutions.[6] The donation of charitable contributions was a public act and was noted with gifts of silver vessels. Giving charity publicly has persisted to today, as the number of plaques naming donors in any Jewish institution will attest.

The drawbacks to the Jews of being an autonomous community became apparent only slowly. Being an autonomous community meant that the Jews would always be considered foreigners, and foreigners resented for their privileges, at that. The Jews didn't pay local taxes, they didn't have to serve in the local militia, and they were given all sorts of trade advantages. The fact that the Jews helped the king meant little in the local communities. The town burghers attacked the Jews by whatever means they could. They restricted Jews from joining town craft guilds, an act that limited Jewish access to many trades. The Jewish quarter, at first a valued privilege, was soon used by the towns to prevent Jews from buying or renting a house or a store anywhere else in town, the modern concept of a ghetto. The Jewish quarter was also a convenient target for riots, riots that usually could be stopped only by the Jews paying the local militia a bribe to protect them. Christian fanatics of all sects hated the Jews because they would not be converted to Christianity. Tsar Michael of Russia in 1638 refused to have any Jews visit Russia, even as representatives of the king of Poland. He wrote, "We never had any Jews in Russia and no Christian may have any intercourse with them."[7] His opinion on the status of Jews was shared by Russian Orthodox, Roman Catholics, Lutherans, and Calvinists alike.

Disaster struck the Jews of Poland in 1648. A horde of Cossacks, Tartars, and Ukrainian peasants revolted against the Polish rule of the Ukraine and defeated the Polish army sent against them. Under the leadership of the chief of the Cossacks, Bogdan Chmelnicki, they raided and looted through the Polish territories pretty much at will for eight years. They saw Jews as one of their prime targets, as the Jews had served their Polish masters as estate managers and tax collectors all too well.[8] Seeing themselves as champions of the Russian Orthodox church, these hordes attacked Jews as "Christ killers" Because these hordes, like all such military hordes, were always in search of loot, they targeted Jewish houses where some portable wealth was likely to be found.

At the same time that Poland was suffering under the Chmelnicki raids, Poland was also involved in a three-cornered war against Sweden and Russia over control of the Baltic coast. Since all armies, Polish, Swedish, or Russian of the time, operated on the principle of making war pay for war, the Jewish communities were subjected to forced contributions again and again as the fortunes of war brought one or another marauding force into town. The Jewish communities never fully recovered their wealth or status. As the kings of Poland, now elected by the nobles, gradually lost power to these nobles and to foreign invaders, the Jews, whose status and privileges the kings had guaranteed, lost power and wealth as well.

These Northern Wars, as they were called, did much damage to the Jewish outlook for the future. The Russians ended up conquering much of the Baltic coast from the Swedes and the Poles, including what today are Latvia and Estonia as well as parts of Finland. Peter the Great built his new capital at the mouth of the Narva River on the Baltic and called it St. Petersburg. In order to win his campaign against the Swedes, Peter had brought in the wild horsemen of the steppes, Kalmucks and Tartars, to harry and burn all villages and farms outside Swedish-held towns. This scorched-earth tactic damaged the wealth of the Jews as well as the Christians. Peter finally defeated the Swedes at the battle of Poltova in the Ukraine and, at the same time, gained the loyalty of the bands of Cossacks as well, or as much loyalty as these wild raiders gave to anyone. Like all the Romanov emperors, Peter based his power partly on the support of the church, a fact that did not augur well for the Jews as well as for any dissidents from Orthodox dogma.

In southeast Europe, the power of the Turkish empire was ebbing. The second Turkish siege of Vienna in 1683 ended in a massive Turkish defeat. Within ten years, the Turks had to cede all of Hungary and Transylvania to the Austrians. The intolerant Romanov and the intolerant Habsburgs continued to press the Turks backward toward Asia until 1918. Since the Turks had been protectors of the Jewish minority, the hatred of the Christians in the

Balkans turned not only on their Muslim oppressors but also on the Jews they had protected.[9]

The outlook for Jews in Western Europe was improving as the outlook in the East deteriorated. The Thirty Years' War ended in 1648. Although it had begun as a religious controversy, religious enthusiasm in Europe was pretty much exhausted during this conflict. Once again Jews were permitted to settle where they had once been banned. In the devastated Rhineland, Jewish cattle traders established orthodox Jewish communities in the villages, and these communities would remain until destroyed by the Holocaust three hundred years later. Frankfurt had its Jewish traders domiciled in the *Judengasse*, or Jewish street.

The rulers of Prussia were seeking new settlers, and Jewish communities were established in Danzig (Gdansk) and Königsberg (Kaleningrad). Since Augustus the Strong of Saxony was also king of Poland, Jewish trading activity in Saxony became possible, and a few wealthy Jews received permission to settle. Most noticeable was the rise of the Jewish communities of Prague and Amsterdam.

Trade to the Orient now travelled by ship rather than overland. At the same time, Holland had gained its independence from Spain, and the eastindiamen, large sailing ships, now travelled between India, the Spice Islands, China, and Holland. Since William of Orange, the ruler of the Netherlands, was also William III of England after 1688, Amsterdam prospered and the Jews prospered with it. Originally Amsterdam had been settled by *Sephardic* Jews from Spain, but gradually *Ashkenazi* were made welcome and employed by the trading houses to travel to the great fairs at Leipzig and Frankfurt. Their knowledge of languages of Eastern Europe and their trade connections in the East made them valuable.[10]

To pay for oriental goods, the eastindiamen carried cargoes of minted silver, silver obtained in part from the mountains of Bohemia. It was this silver that was first minted into the large *Joachimsthaler* in 1520. This coin in turn served as the pattern for all European talers, dollars, and crowns, which were the standard European currency until 1933. Jews became mint masters to many of the princes of Europe, and the Jewish community of Prague became wealthy from the profits of the Bohemian silver mines. Since Western Europe became more prosperous and open to Jews and Eastern Europe less so, immigration began to flow from east to west, reversing the pattern of the previous centuries.

With the dying out of the Jagellon dynasty and the change of the crown of Poland to an elective office, the position of king of Poland had become a prize to be won by bribery for the candidates of the tsar, the princes of Saxony, and by interference from all the other nations of Europe. Finally Poland's three neighbors, Russia, Prussia, and Austria, decided to divide up Poland between themselves. There were partitions of Poland in 1773, 1779, and 1793. The attempt by the Poles to resist the Russians led by Kosziusko, who had served in the American Revolution under Washington, was unavailing. The Jews, understanding well that their future was also at stake, had supported the Polish freedom movement. When the royal robbers divided up the spoil, Prussia, under Frederick the Great, got the province of Silesia, including Wroclaw (Breslau) and Poznanz (Posen). The Jews in those provinces were now considered German Jews. The Austrians, under Maria Theresa, the patron of the young Mozart, took Galicia, including the cities of Lodz (Lemberg, Litzmannstadt) and the trading town of Brody. When final adjustments were made after the defeat of Napoleon in 1815, Russia ended up with the lion's share, including what today is Lithuania, Byelarus, the Ukraine, and the central part of Poland including Warsaw. A few special concessions were made to the Poles in that the tsar ruled as king of Poland, but that did not change the fact of the annexation itself. Poland, as a state, disappeared from the maps of Europe for 100 years.

The Jewish communities survived the change of rulers as best they could and in many ways, especially in language and customs, maintained a unity of culture in Eastern Europe despite the new borders.

All of the new rulers still treated the Jews as a corporate entity, not as individuals and citizens. Catherine II, the German princess who had become tsarina of Russia, limited her new Jewish subjects to a Pale of Settlement in which they could live, a territory confined to the old Polish provinces. When Tsar Nicholas I wanted to draft Jews into his conscript army in 1827, he left it to the leaders of the kahillas to choose which unfortunate boys were to put on a uniform and to swear them into the tsar's service with solemn religious oaths and ceremonies.[11] Taxes were levied on the Jewish community at large, and it was left to the elders to apportion the burden. It was not until 1859 that individual rich merchants, doctors, lawyers, and other university graduates were allowed to leave the Pale of Settlement and move to St. Petersburg, Moscow, and other cities. Of course they were still prohibited from becoming government officials or rising as officers in the army.

The kahillas and rabbis continued to control the ghettos, their schools, and their markets. The few attempts to establish for Jews in Russian Poland government schools with a more modern curriculum and Russian language instruction failed, as did a similar effort to establish such schools in the Austrian Galicia.[12]

The situation of the Jews in Galicia was just as oppressed as in tsarist Russia. The Edict of Toleration published by the emperor, Joseph II, in 1789 meant what it said, bare toleration rather than any equality of Jews and Christians. Jews were prohibited from living in villages in Galicia unless they were engaged in either agriculture or handicrafts. They were prohibited from engaging in trade, operating taverns, leasing mills, or collecting tolls. This edict was not always enforced, but the threat of enforcement always hung over every Jew living in a Galician village.

The Austrian government did recognize Jews as individuals or as households rather than as part of a corporate community when it came to paying taxes. Ritually slaughtered meat was heavily taxed, and there was a tax on sabbath candles. Each married Jewish woman had to pay taxes on two sabbath candles a week, whether she had money to buy candles or not. The tax was enforced under the threat of forfeiture of all household goods. Leaders of the kahilla were forced to prove that they had paid taxes on six or eight sabbath candles rather than just two before they could assume office, a regulation that ensured that only wealthy Jews could be elected to community leadership.[13]

At the same time, restrictions on residence outside legally defined ghettos were introduced in major cities, and Jews were not allowed to live in some towns at all. Very rich Jews or those possessing university degrees were exempt from these residence restrictions, here as in Russia.

Prussia proved to be the most liberal of the gainers from the partition of Poland. As part of the reforms instituted in Prussia to oppose Napoleon, an edict was issued on March 11, 1812, that gave full citizenship to Jews in Prussia together with the formal removal of all residence and professional restrictions. These new laws applied to native-born Jews only; foreign, that is, Russian, Jews still suffered from restrictions.[14] This division between native and foreign Jews was of importance then and still exists in present-day German law as it did in the days of the German empire, the Weimar Republic, and the Nazi regime.

To show how difficult it is to separate the Ashkenazic Jews into German and Eastern groups, the results of the Prussian census of 1863 are of interest. The province of Posen (Posnanz) had 74,172 Jews. Silesia counted 40,856 Jews, and East Prussia, including Danzig (Gdansk) and Königsberg (Kaleningrad), counted 37,635 Jewish residents. All Brandenburg, which included Berlin, Saxony, Pomerania, Westphalia and the Rhineland combined, had only 79,836 Jews. Therefore, Jews in the former Poland outnumbered Jews in the rest of Prussia by about two to one.[15] Of course there were also Jews in Baden, Bavaria, and Würtemberg.

The Prussian and later the German government still dealt with the kahillas in many affairs rather than with individual Jews. It collected the Jewish community membership dues at the same time as the income tax and in turn paid out a subsidy to the Jewish communities for religious and charitable purposes. This is still the law today; the various Jewish synagogues and communities are supported by government funds and the kahilla in turn allocates the lump sums to the various congregations and agencies. As a result elections to the kahilla boards were and are fiercely contested.[16]

When the Nazis rose to power, they revived many of the old evils. Restrictions on Jews owning businesses or entering certain professions were instituted, ghettos were reestablished, and special taxes were placed on the Jewish community at large rather than on individuals. The new ghettos were governed by Nazi-appointed Jewish officials, the *Judenrat*, right up to the point when the entire ghettos were "cleansed" and the inhabitants either shot out of hand or deported to extermination camps. Like the tsars of 100 years earlier, the Nazis made the Jewish officials pick who was to be deported first. Eventually, of course, the Jewish councillors and policemen shared the fate of their ghetto, but each of these officials had to make the difficult choice between cooperating with the Nazis in the hope of saving some or preparing to go down fighting.[17]

In the middle of the eighteenth and early nineteenth century, a popular revival movement, the *Hasidim*, the Pietists, swept through the Jewish population of Galicia, the Ukraine, and Poland. The Hasidim believed that certain men were *zaddiks*, "just" or "holy" men whose holiness came from the spirit rather than from a study of the Jewish writings. These charismatic personalities became the supreme authority in the communities of their adherents. The zaddik was seen as an intermediary between the ordinary Jew and the Deity. Of course, most of the Hasidic leaders were also learned in Torah and Talmud.

The effect of Hasidism on Jewish life in the eastern Jewish areas was enormous, even on those who were not followers of the zaddiks. Since Hasidism placed emphasis on the spirit of worship rather than on details of ritual, the poor Jew who did not know all of the ritual or prayers could now feel himself to be an equal of the leaders of the synagogue or those wealthy enough to be formal yeshiva students. Wealth was no longer the only factor that made a "good Jew," and partly for that reason, Hasidism had its strongest appeal among the Jewish lower classes.

The use of Yiddish as a language rather than a variety of dialects was also spread by Hasidic publications, which passed from region to region. Pamphlets and even prayer books were in Yiddish among the Hasidim rather than in the scholar's Hebrew or the government's German, Russian, or Polish. The sayings of the zaddiks, the old folktales, and many of the pithy expressions that have been absorbed into the slang of Berlin, New York, and Hollywood are passed down to us through the Hasidim. It was nearly a hundred years after the origin of Hasidic writings in Yiddish that authors like Mendele, Peretz, and Sholem Aleichem created what is now called "Yiddish literature," and even then, many of their stories deal with the Hasids rather than the more scholarly rabbis.

Another effect of this movement was to increase the amount of travel among the Jews. Every Hasid tried to spend at least some time at the residence of his zaddik, often located at a considerable distance away from his home village. Up to this time only merchants, scholars, and coachmen travelled beyond the borders of their own and a few neighboring villages. Now it became more common for even a poor man to have visited another town, even though it might be quite similar to his own. This tendency to travel increased even more with the coming of the railroads. This acceptance of travel was to have a considerable influence on the ability of Jews in the nineteenth century to migrate to any major city and find people from their home town or region who would help them acclimate. Clusters of people from a specific town or region who helped each other existed even before the formation of the formal *Landsmannschaften*, or regional associations.

Naturally this new religious movement of the Hasids did not go unchallenged. The traditional rabbis and synagogues considered the Hasids heretics to be excommunicated and driven out of the community of Jews. The center of the resistance to Hasidism and stronghold of the *mishnagadim*, or Opponents, was the Jewish community of the city of Vilna. In sermons and writings, the traditional orthodox rabbis accused the Hasidim of discouraging the study of the sacred writings, of interjecting "obnoxious foreign words," that is, Yiddish, into the prayers, and, in their exuberance, of turning "head over heels" during the services.[18] The Hasidim were even blamed for an epidemic among the children of Vilna in 1771, the rabbis claiming that the Deity had sent the plague as a punishment for the appearance of this heresy.[19] Besides proclaiming a solemn excommunication against the Hasidim in Vilna, they also sent letters asking authorities in other Jewish communities to take similar stern measures. These exhortations were not altogether unsuccessful. The town of Brody, for instance, saw the rabbis proclaim a similar excommunication of Hasids in May 1772. The Hasids retaliated in kind. In Galicia they intimated that only meat slaughtered by Hasidic ritual slaughterers was truly *kosher* and only circumcisions carried out by Hasidic *mohels* were truly valid. They accused the kahilla and its officers of a wide range of ritual transgressions.[20]

Despite the name calling between the two groups of orthodox Jews, the Jewish communities were not truly disrupted. Partly this came about because a third movement of a different Judaism arose at the same time as Hasidism. This was the *Haskala*, or the enlightenment. This movement originated in Germany, fostered by Moses Mendelssohn and David Friedlander. They held that Judaism is a religion like other religions and was neither a culture nor a nationality. Therefore it would be perfectly proper, they believed, for Jews to learn to speak the language of their Christian neighbors and to dress like them. These ideas of enlightenment had their greatest impact among the Jewish upper classes, the doctors, lawyers, and merchants who were in daily contact with their Christian neighbors.

All three of these branches of Judaism claimed that they represented Judaism at its best, although they always recognized that the members of all three branches were Jews, unlike the schisms among Christians. They made shifting alliances with each other depending on the particular issue at hand. The Hasids and traditionalists united in calling the followers of the enlightenment "assimilationists," but the followers of the enlightenment were at one with the traditionalists in opposing the use of Yiddish which they called "jargon."[21]

The controversies between the branches of Judaism have not completely subsided among the Jews of today. The official head of the Jews in Germany, Mr. Bubis, was horrified when the Jewish community of Oldenburg hired a female rabbi, and swore never to set foot in that synagogue while she officiated. The *Harredim*, the modern very orthodox Jews, attack a less religious government of the state of Israel for violating ritual by allowing archaeological excavations, and they also try to impose the orthodox Jewish ideas about education and advertising in Israel. In New York, it is impossible to distinguish most Jews from their non-Jewish neighbors by dress or appearance, but some Jews walk about the streets dressed in the costume of nineteenth-century Poland. There have been some general compromises. Jewish religious schools of all groups devote half of their teaching day to secular subjects, an idea first proposed by David Friedlander in Berlin and rejected with horror by the traditionalists of the time. Despite all the differences, all Jews today consider themselves to be members of one religion and one community if they consider themselves to be Jews at all.

To get a clearer idea of how the eastern Jewish communities functioned and what ideas were transferred westward, it is wise to examine more than the religious and governmental structure. To try to visualize the world of eastern Jewry, we will examine the period of the 1840s.

The basic unit of the Jewish world, whether in a village, a small town, or the Jewish quarter of a big city, was the family. In a Jewish house the women were in charge of the home. They saw to the comforts, the running of the house, and the raising of small children. This is clearly recognized in Jewish ritual, where it is the women who say the blessing over the sabbath candles. The women also played a role in the economics of the household, not only supervising the budget to a considerable extent but also often running a small store located in the front room of the residence. The Victorian idea that women were to be shielded from money matters never caught on in Jewish circles. Women also served as midwives and prepared the bodies of women for burial. Men were not expected to help in the housework, and a widower with small children was considered to be totally helpless in the house. He was an object of pity and was encouraged to remarry as soon as possible. Bachelors were also considered to be helpless, and women brought them food or darned their clothes.

The man dealt with everything outside of the house. He was expected to carry on a craft or have an occupation. At the same time, he was expected to study the sacred writings and to discuss the affairs of the synagogue with the other men. No woman had a vote in the kahilla. A man could raise his social status by being learned or by marrying the daughter of a rich merchant or a rabbi. The marriage of a poor but learned yeshiva student with the daughter of a rich merchant was considered the ideal by both parties, though if the man also had money, that was even better. Girls, on the other hand, derived their social status from the position of their fathers or their husbands rather than from their own accomplishments, though they were expected to be skilled in household tasks and were, preferably, good-looking. Under these circumstances, the marriage broker, who was expected to know everything about everybody in the community, was a necessary and respected figure.

Children were desired, and a barren woman or a girl who died before having children was considered a special tragedy. However, boys were preferred to girls. Only boys could say the prayers for the deceased parents, and boys would carry on the family name. Girls had to be provided with dowries, money that would pass out of the family possession into that of the husband. Dowries were so important that religious charitable societies existed in every community to provide dowries for the poor and orphaned girls. Boys, on the other hand, brought the dowries of their brides into the family treasury. Marriage contracts specified the exact amount and kind of dowry the bride would bring with her.

There was considerable age grading, among both boys and girls. The oldest boy was "ransomed" in the synagogue, a ceremony deriving from the practice of ancient Israel of dedicating the firstborn of all kinds to the Deity. Younger sons had a lower status, and it was the eldest son who would become the head of the household upon the death of the father. Among the daughters of the house, age grading meant that they were expected to marry in strict order of age. An older sister who had difficulty finding a husband for reasons of health, looks, or personality was therefore a hindrance to all her family, and every effort was made to marry her off as quickly as possible. If necessary, this was done by increasing the amount of her dowry. The size of the dowry and the splendor of the wedding of the oldest was the source of considerable tension. Great expenditure would increase the *yikkus*, or reputation, of the family and might attract more suitors for the other girls. On the other hand, if too much money was expended for the first wedding, there would be little left for the younger sisters. Occasionally a girl, especially a younger daughter, would make a love match regardless of social position, and lesbianism was not unknown.[22]

Learning made for high status, regardless of whether it was acquired in a yeshiva or a secular university. Money in itself was less of a factor than money donated publicly in charity or spent in conspicuous consumption.

Yikkus was a family matter, so the doings of any member of the family reflected on all, and family members felt justified in calling an errant member to account. Many of these traits can still be found in the customs of some Jewish families, though their importance is much diminished.

Jews had a well-defined fear of government, any and all governments, a fear based on experience. Officials of all kinds in Eastern Europe expected gifts or favors from petitioners. Therefore it was considered wiser not to call oneself to the attention of any authority figure. Compromise was sought after, if necessary by involving a respected arbitrator. This was one of the roles of the rabbi, in addition to assisting in cases requiring discreet charity or help.

As far as possible, Jewish communities were self-sufficient. Food was bought from other Jews at the market or in small stores.

There were Jewish blacksmiths and wheelwrights, leather workers and shoemakers, tailors and dressmakers. Jewish doctors and law-yers were preferred to non-Jews, but since they operated outside of the traditional Jewish community, they were not really trusted and only brought in as a last resort.

Special mention should be made of the *luftmenschen*, the people who "lived by air." These were not truly unemployed, but rather men who had no special profession and dabbled in anything and everything. They bought or sold anything, from a goat to a gold pin, either on their own account or for a small commission. They might help a carter load his wagon or help the teacher by carrying small boys to school. They brought water from the well or helped chop timber for a contractor. Many successful Jewish businessmen were simply lucky luftmenschen, jewelers who dabbled in real estate or contractors turned traders or manufacturers.

Almost all men and many women were literate, at least in Yiddish. Books, pamphlets, and newspapers circulated in the Jew-ish communities, even if often at second or third hand. News and international affairs were discussed even in the villages, the infor-mation coming not only from printed material but also from mail or visits from relatives living far away. National borders meant little in a world where those borders shifted often. To use Vilna as an example once more, the city was Russian in 1914, occupied by the German army in 1915–1918, fought over by White and Red armies in 1919, and was then part of Lithuania, Central Lithuania, and finally Poland. In 1939 it became Russian once more, then German, then Russian, and now Lithuanian once more. The shifting borders make national patriotism a difficult concept.

Not all Jews lived in Jewish communities. Though admission in Russian universities was limited by quota, some Jews could and did attend them. Medicine was the most popular subject of study. Those Jews who could not get into Russian universities tried to get into German or Austrian schools.[23] Some of these students from foreign universities returned to the Jewish communities, but many stayed in the large cities of the West. The richer merchants also often left Jewish communities to settle in St. Petersburg, Moscow, Kiev, or elsewhere. Factory owners were travellers too, but many such owners remained, building factories in the areas of Jewish settlement and drawing many of their workers from Jewish communities.

We shall examine later in this book the migrants from the Jewish upper classes and the ideas they carried westward as well as the role of the poor, who were forced out of the Jewish communities of the East by economic need or government oppression.

NOTES

1. For the purposes of this book, the term "Eastern Europe" includes Belarus, Latvia, Lithuania, Poland, Russia west of the Volga River, and the Ukraine except for the Crimea; Hungary, Romania, and Moldova have a different political history than the rest of Eastern Europe but share many cultural characteristics with the other Jews of Eastern Europe. The Jews of Bulgaria, Greece, and Serbia are mostly of Sephardic rather than Ashkenazic origin.

2. Israel Cohen, *Vilna* (Philadelphia: Jewish Publication Society, 1943), p. 8.

3. Rudolf Schramil, *Stadtverfassung nach Magdeburger Recht*, ed. Dr. Otto von Gierke (Breslau: Untersuchungen der Staats-und-Rechtsgeschichte, Heft 125, 1915).

4. Cohen, p. 17.

5. For an example of such an accusation and its consequences, see: Michael Cohn, *Medieval Justice: The Trial of the Jews of Trent* (New York: Yeshiva University Museum, 1989).

6. Cohen, p. 116.

7. Ibid., p. 35.

8. Bernard Pares, *A History of Russia* (New York: Knopf, 1928), p. 167.

9. Anti-Semitism is strong in most of the Balkans. The hatred of the Moslems is still a major factor in the Bosnia conflict of today and is current in Bulgaria and Greece as well.

10. The catalogue of the silverwork in the Jewish museum in Amsterdam shows physical evidence of migration, and it is documented in much of the literature as well.

11. The old Yiddish folk song ran:

> Our leaders and our rabbis
> Even help give them away for the Gentiles.
> Rich Zushe Rakover has seven sons
> But not one puts on the uniform.

Zvi Gitelman, *A Century of Ambivalence* (New York: YIVO Institute for Jewish Research, 1988), p. 6.

12. Raphael Mahler, *Hasidism and Jewish Enlightenment* (Philadelphia: Jewish Publication Society, 1985), pp. 7–8.

13. Ibid., p. 25.

14. Bilderarchiv Preussicher Kulturbesitz, *Juden in Preussen* (Dortmund: Hardenberg Kommunikation, 1981), pp. 170–171.

15. Ibid.

16. In 1995 the election to the board of the kahilla of Hanover was disputed and the charge was made that Russian Jewish immigrants were allowed to vote before they had even been registered in the community.

17. Besides the well-known uprising of the Warsaw ghetto, there were also armed uprisings at the extermination camp of Sobidor and the work camp at Bendsburg near Katowice.

18. Cohen, p. 237.

19. Mahler, p. 25.

20. Ibid.

21. In a letter of 1822, a father wrote to his son, "Why use the Judeo-German language in the land of Poland? Use either the holy tongue or Polish." Ibid., p. 39.

In a survey of the Jews of Munich in 1902, Yiddish was still listed as "Jargon." Brigitte Scheiger, "Juden in Berlin," in *Von Zuwanderern zu Einheimischen*, ed. Barbara John and Stefi Jersch-Wenzel (Berlin: Nicolai, 1990).

22. Shalom Aleichem, "A Daughter's Grave," in Aleichem's *In the Old Country* (New York: Crown Publishers, 1946), p. 238.

23. Rachel Salamander, ed., *Jewish World of Yesterday 1860–1938* (New York: Rizzoli International Publishers, 1991), p. 113. For Berlin and Königsberg, see Scheiger, p. 407.

2

Pressures on Eastern European Jewry

Jewish communities in Eastern Europe came under increasing pressure from about 1840 on. These pressures were economic and cultural—and finally threatened their lives as well.

The Industrial Revolution that had begun in Britain in the 1780s arrived in Russia and Poland some seventy years later. As in Britain, newly established large textile factories drove the hand weavers out of business. In Eastern Europe a few Jewish hand weavers of prayer shawls managed to maintain themselves. The coming of the railroads deprived coachmen, carters, and bargemen of their livelihoods, although some river traffic of bulk cargo and timber still remained. The coming of the sewing machine in the 1850s and the ready-made clothing made by these machines reduced tailors and dressmakers in the small towns to doing only repairs and alterations. Shoemakers were reduced to being cobblers by machine-produced boots. These old professions were trades that had sustained the Jewish economy in the villages and small towns for centuries. Now they all disappeared as means of making a respectable living.

Industrialization is a social as well as an economic change. Work is regularized and disciplined. In the alien environment of the factory, there is no place for the small comforts enjoyed by the domestic worker, the brief nap to compensate for a poor night's sleep, the pleasure of observing children at play, the spontaneous affection between husband and wife.[1] Nor is there time to stop for prayers or for ceasing work on religious holidays and the sabbath. Machines make money for their owners only if they are kept going constantly.

The comprehensive welfare system that had been adequate for the small *stetl* could not handle the load of problems that affected the Jews in a large city. There was little role for the old, small children, or the sick in the world based on the factory. Yet economic activity and opportunity for young workers were much better in the cities, and the young migrated to them. Often the old parents and the young siblings were left behind in the villages, but the Jewish population of the cities kept growing. At the turn of the century, 32 percent of the population of Warsaw was Jewish. The proportion of Jews in Lublin was even higher.[2] It is estimated that there were 300,000 Jewish industrial workers, of whom 50,000 actually worked in factories. In Bialystok, for instance, all the workers in the lumber mills, machine shops, and tobacco plants were Jews, as were the workers in the pig-bristle factories.[3] The Jews not working in the factories ran stores in the cities, were porters and van drivers, and worked in all the establishments that were needed to support the population of the factories.

The Jews, for the first time in history, formed part of the proletariat. As a result these Jews soon saw themselves as having more in common with their fellow workers than with the people of their home towns. By 1897 they organized the *Allgemeiner Yiddisher Arbeiterbund*, the Jewish Workers League, commonly simply called the Bund. However, there had already been strikes in the Lodz textile factories before the Bund was organized in 1895. Originally the Bund had been part of the Russian Social Democratic Labor party, but it was expelled from that party in 1903 for "nationalist positions." It was the first but hardly the last conflict between the role of the Jews as workers and their role as Jews.

The Bund sought "cultural national autonomy," an idea first formulated by the Austrian socialist leader Otto Bauer. It opposed both religious orthodoxy and Zionism.[4]

Of course, not all Jews living in the major cities were proletarians. There was also a small strata of upper-class Jewish merchants and professionals and a larger body of bourgeois storekeepers and craftsmen. There was also a Jewish *lumpenproletariat*, Jews on the bottom of the economic heap struggling to survive as porters, drivers of horse cabs, and professional beggars.

Another source of pressure on the Jewish communities of Eastern Europe was overpopulation. Jewish men often married in their midteens. Children, many children, were sought after, preferably boys. Children were the insurance of financial help in old age, and a son might go to America and send back money. The youngest daughter would often stay home, unmarried or married late, to take care of elderly parents. A barren woman or a spinster, though, was a blot on the family reputation. Marriage brokers sought wide-hipped girls who could bear children easily and looked with suspicion on slender, frail girls who might not be up to the physical burden of caring for a large family. In this way the Jewish ideal differed from the sylphlike females who were the ideal of the Victorian West.

At the same time, medical advances in the nineteenth century dramatically cut mortality rates. The vaccination for smallpox, antiseptics, and the invention of forceps allowed more women and babies to survive, although typhus, typhoid, diphtheria, and tuberculosis remained serious threats to life in Eastern Europe until the advent of antibiotics after World War II. After the break-up of the Soviet Union, typhoid, diphtheria, and tuberculosis have reappeared in Russia, and the average life span for men has dropped to 55.

Emigration to Western Europe and the United States became first a trickle, then a stream, and finally a flood, but the Jewish population of Russia remained fairly constant at five million. Even today, after the Holocaust and the reduction of the geographic size of Russia, it is estimated that there are still two to three million Jews living within the borders of Russia, Byelarus, and the Ukraine.

In addition to the pressures of industrialization and overpopulation, the Jewish communities in the East were exposed to ever-increasing government attacks. In 1827, as has already been noted, Tsar Nicholas I of Russia, called the "Iron Tsar," imposed a draft of soldiers on the Jewish communities. The period of service in the Russian army was twenty-five years. In order to avoid drafting husbands and fathers, the Jewish community leaders sent boys as young as twelve to be trained as soldiers until they reached the statutory age of eighteen, at which time their twenty-five years of service would begin. These *cantonists* seldom if ever saw their homes again. In addition to the high death rate from unsanitary conditions in the barracks and the harsh climate, which killed off many of the weaker boys, the recruits were put under tremendous pressure to convert to Russian Orthodox Christianity. The tsars saw themselves as champions of the Russian Orthodox Church and believed that belonging to this faith would help unify Russia. Therefore, priests were offered rewards for converting not only Jews but also Lutherans and other "unbelievers" and schismatics to the "proper faith." Campaigns of repression were waged against the Roman Catholic Poles, the Baltic Germans, and the "Old Believers" just as much as against the Jewish communities. All schools were forced to use Russian as the language for instruction and put under Russian officials chosen for their belief in Russianization.

This was also a period of Russian expansion in Asia and the fostering of pan-Slavism in Europe. After conquering the Caucasus in 1869, the Turcomen were beaten in 1881 by the Russian army, and their territory was occupied. The old Mohammedan strongholds of Khiva and Samarkand as well as Bokhara were stormed and made into protectorates in the 1870s. The lands along the Amur River in Siberia were taken from China in the so-called Unequal Treaties. To integrate all of these new subjects, the Russian language and the Russian church plus the resettlement of Russians were used as tools.

In Europe, Russia extended its influence by going to war against Turkey in 1877 and forcing Turkey to grant Romania, Serbia, and Bulgaria independence, naturally expecting these countries to remain in the Russian political orbit. This policy worked to the detriment of the Jewish population of these countries. The tsar made it clear to the British government that he considered himself to be the guardian of all Christians in Turkish lands.[5] This policy was one of the causes of World War I.

The Austrian government followed a similar course to that of the Russians: imperialism in the Balkans coupled with a policy of Germanification, especially in regard to the Jews of Galicia. This attempt to make Galicia more "German" and therefore a strong frontier against Russia served as justification for anti-Jewish policies. By 1810 every Jew who wanted to vote in the kahilla elections had to prove his proficiency in German. By 1814 it was decreed that no documents in Hebrew or Yiddish could be introduced in the courts as evidence. In 1820 it was decreed that all synagogue services were to be conducted in German or "in a local language."[6]

Russian governmental pressure on the Jews relaxed a bit under the more liberally inclined Tsar Alexander II (1855–1880) but his assassination by left-wing radicals in 1881 was a signal for massive pogroms launched by groups claiming to be against liberalism and against the Jews as "anti-Russian." Mobs roamed through the Jewish quarters of many towns, looting and killing. Perhaps only a few hundred lives were lost, which is few in comparison with the later excesses, but the self-confidence of the Jewish community and their hopes of a future progressive and tolerant Russia were shattered. The police had stood by while the mobs rampaged, doing nothing to stop the outrages. Even the Russian social radicals issued a statement approving of the pogroms.[7] From this time on, very few Jews saw a good future for themselves in tsarist Russia. This hopeless future was made even clearer to them when the pogroms were followed by decrees driving the Jews from the land and establishing quotas at the universities and high schools, limiting admission to otherwise qualified Jews. Thousands of Jews fled Russia any way they could. By the summer of 1881, refugees were pouring into the Galician border city of Brody. There were 20,000 refugees clustered in and around a city with a normal population of 15,000.[8] Other Jews tried to flee into Prussia or even Hungary.

The pogroms of October 1905 were even more widespread and severe than those of 1880. This time the police, instead of idly standing by, took an active role in organizing and helping in these "spontaneous" demonstrations. About 900 Jews died and about 100,000 suffered personal or economic injuries. Pictures of the rows of Jewish dead and the injured were sent to the Jewish communities of the West, some of them by Jewish organizations trying to raise relief funds.[9] These pictures, coupled with those of "Bloody Sunday," when troops fired on peaceful demonstrators in St. Petersburg in February 1905, convinced many Westerners, Jewish and non-Jewish, that Russia was living in the dark ages. The Cossacks were equated with the savage warriors of Ghengis Khan and Attilla the Hun. Fear of the Cossacks became established not only among the Jews but also among the Germans living near the Russian frontier. In 1914 the Imperial German General Staff shifted two army corps to East Prussia from the Western Front, where they were sorely missed at the Battle of the Marne.[10] The Jews of Galicia fled wildly from the advancing Russian armies that same winter, and the German army was successful when they claimed to come as the liberators of the Jews as they entered Russian Poland.[11]

The events of the Russian civil war of 1917–1921 proved that the Jewish fear of the Cossacks had a basis in fact. The Don Cossacks, allied with the White Army of General Denikin in southern Russia, staged pogroms that caused the death of thousands of Jews. The Ukrainian nationalist forces of Semen Petliura also engaged in pogroms. Again waves of Jewish emigrants travelled westward to escape death.[12]

The Eastern Jews who flooded into western cities formed their own neighborhoods, which resembled the stetls of Poland and

Russia. In Berlin this Eastern Jewish section was the *Scheunen-viertel*, the barn district, a slum located behind the *Alexanderplatz* in the center of the city. In Vienna the Eastern Jewish district was the Second District, near the banks of the Danube. In London the Jews settled in the East End beyond the Tower of London. The most famous of these settlements was the Lower East Side in New York City. All of these districts were near the centers of the cities, where work might be obtained.[13]

Between 1880 and 1914, an estimated 2.5 million Jews left Russia. This is in addition to the Jewish emigration from Galicia and Romania as well as Silesia and German Poland. Approximately 1.5 million of these Eastern Jews came to the United States.[14] Jews from the East in the 1920s were, to a large extent, blocked from entering the United States by the new immigration laws of 1921 and 1924, and therefore they settled in western European ghettos.

Some of the Russian and Polish Jews were able to move east instead of west when the Russian government in 1915 ordered the border districts cleared of Jewish inhabitants as a security measure. The German propaganda had proved effective. The clearing of the Russian border districts in turn meant the abandonment of the Jewish Pale of Settlement that had existed since the days of Catherine the Great in the eighteenth century. Jews now were allowed to live in the cities of all of Russia. Other Jews stayed in the territories that were included in the new republics of Latvia, Lithuania, and Poland established after World War I. In these countries, the old stetl life continued until the coming of the Nazis in 1939.

Many Jews became communists during the time of the Russian civil war. Some of these individuals were already Marxists and gradually moved from socialism to communism out of conviction. Others, like Trotsky, born Bronstein, were communists right from the beginning. The behavior of the Whites of the counterrevolutionary armies convinced many others that their only chance of life lay with the Red Army and the Bolsheviks.

The Bolsheviks welcomed Jews as individuals but were not interested in fostering either Jewish religion or Jewish culture.

Lenin had made his position clear in an article written in 1909. "Dialectic materialism is absolutely atheistic and definitely hostile to all religions," he wrote.[15] At the same time, he warned that to preach atheism at all times and under all circumstances was only to play into the hand of the church and the priests.

The concept of Jewish cultural activity as separate from religion fared no better in the minds of the Communist leadership. "As to the project of a so-called national-cultural autonomy which should unite the Jews throughout the whole country around schools and other institutions," wrote Trotsky, "this reactionary utopia borrowed by various Jewish groups from the Austrian theoretician Otto Bauer melted like wax during the first days of freedom."[16] Some of the melting of these ideas was due to the fire supplied by the Bolshevik Central Committee. The Bund and the various socialist-inclined Zionist groups were forced to merge into the Communist party. Mindful of Lenin's advice, a Jewish section was maintained through the Committee of Nationalities under Stalin. This Jewish section under the leadership of Esther Frumkin, a former Bundist, was allowed to lead the attack on Jewish religion and the Hebrew language, which was part of the general antireligious campaign of the Bolsheviks during the 1920s. During this time synagogues were turned into movie houses, the sacred writings were burned, and the silver Torah ornaments melted down for the benefit of the state treasury. There was a let-up of this campaign during the days of Lenin's New Economic Policy, but in 1927 Stalin dissolved the Jewish section of the Communist party. Most of the leaders of this section were arrested during the purges of the 1930s by Stalin's secret police and either summarily shot or sent to the gulags after a show trial. Zionism, of course, was always fought by the Communists as "bourgeois nationalism," that is, as being against the interests of the Russian state. Pure anti-Semitism, attacks on Jews as Jews, occurred only much later during the so-called doctors trials of 1952. However, the large number of Jews in the original Central Committee, such as Trotsky and Radek, had been eliminated in the 1920s and put on trial in the 1930s as counterrevolutionaries.

Jewish intellectuals such as the ethnologist Simon Dubnow and the painter Chagall emigrated, as did the Jewish Habima theater group. Some intellectuals, like Ilya Ehrenburg, and politicians, like Maxim Litvinov (Meir Wallach), although Jews, managed to survive the zigs and zags of Soviet policy. A few Yiddish newspapers survived in one form or another, as did the Jewish Autonomous Territory of Birobidzhan founded in 1924, but in these cases, frequent purges of the leadership led to the loss of knowledge of Jewish traditions and religion in Soviet Russia. However, the nationality "Jew" was still stamped in Soviet passports as long as the Soviet regime lasted.[17]

When the Communist state started to dissolve in the 1980s, another wave of Jews left Russia for Western countries. The Zionist organizations made every effort to direct these Russians to settle in Israel, but many of them settled instead in New York. Russian immigrants in Germany have revitalized many Jewish communities there. The Russian and Ukrainian Jews, together with smaller groups of Jews from Uzbekistan, Kazakhstan and Tajikstan, now form the majority of the Jews in Germany. For the moment, Russian has replaced German as the conversational language among Jews, although the next generation will undoubtedly speak German. This Russian immigration is strongly resented by other Jews in Germany, and its impact on the Jewish culture of Germany remains to be seen.[18]

The most overwhelming event to strike the Eastern Jews is, of course, the happenings that are included under the term "Holocaust." In October 1938, a month before the notorious *Kristallnacht*, the Nazi government of Germany expelled all Jews who held Polish passports. This included many Jews who had lived in Germany for more than a generation but had been unable to obtain German citizenship. They were rounded up and dumped into open fields at the Polish border. It took the Polish government three days to decide to admit these "Poles" into Poland as citizens while others were returned to Germany.

Less than a year later, the German army occupied all of Poland west of the Bug River, the Soviet army taking over the rest of Poland, almost all of Lithuania, all of Latvia, and Estonia. The extermination of the native Jews began immediately, often with the help of the local population.[19]

All of the Jews in German-occupied Poland were forced into ghettos, some in large cities like Warsaw, Lublin, and Lodz[20] and some in smaller towns like Deblin.[21] Factories making use of Jewish slave labor were established in or near the ghettos to supply goods for the German army. At this time it was the official German presumption that most of the Jews would die of starvation and disease, those Jews not able to work dying quicker because they got less rations. Killings were on a somewhat casual basis at this time.[22]

The situation deteriorated rapidly in 1941 on orders from Berlin.[23] Transports of the very young, the old, and the weak were organized. These individuals were sent to the extermination camps, where the Germans experimented with methods of producing the most efficient methods of mass murder. Many of the ghetto factories were also relocated to the camps.[24] At the same time transports dumped Jews from Berlin and Frankfurt, Vienna, Paris, and Amsterdam into the overcrowded ghettos. These Westernized Jews were doubly helpless, being victimized by the Germans and totally unfamiliar with the basic Eastern Jewish organization of the ghettos. Many ghettos were "liquidated," while some, like the Warsaw ghetto, managed to resist. Others survived the war, as did many of the camps. This does not mean that most of the individuals in these ghettos or camps survived. Most Jews died or were transported to die in the gas ovens of the extermination camps.

When the German army struck at Russia in June 1941, the Germans no longer bothered with the establishment of ghettos, the selection of slave labor, or even extermination camps. Special execution squads, called *Extrakommando* or *Sonderkommando*, were organized, using second-line German troops together with Lithuanian, Ukrainian, or Estonian auxiliary units, all commanded by SS officers. In town after town, the Jewish quarters were surrounded and the Jews marched out to a convenient patch of woods or the edge of a ravine. There they were ordered to strip, shot in the head or heart, and dumped into shallow graves.[25] A few Jews managed to flee with the retreating Soviet troops. A few more managed to maintain themselves as partisans in the forests, but most of the Jews of Byelarus, the Ukraine, eastern Poland, and western Russia died. Their synagogues and their books were burned. Only the more acculturated Jews living in Russian cities beyond the reach of the German army survived World War II.

After the war, some of the Jewish survivors in Poland returning from camps or from hiding tried to reestablish their communities. The attempt was a failure, partly because the survivors were too few and the family pattern was disrupted. The mostly younger, single individuals could not make a community. Also, the Poles organized a series of pogroms in Poland, which sent almost all of the surviving Polish Jewry fleeing across the German border to the displaced persons camps that had been established by the Western Allies.[26] When these were closed down in 1948, many of the Jews emigrated to Israel and the United States. Some, however, remained in Germany and now form much of the leadership of the Jews in Germany.[27]

Since 1989, the Jews living in the West have tried to revive Jewish cultural and religious life in Russia. They have sent visiting rabbis, prayer books, and matzohs as well as financial support. Now the umbrella group of the Jews in Russia is trying to free itself from Western support and create its own form of Jewish culture in Russia. What form this will take remains to be seen.[28]

NOTES

1. John W. Osborne, *The Silent Revolution* (New York: Scribner's, 1970), p. 39.

2. Salamander, p. 85.

3. Working with pig bristles did not violate Jewish religious laws as long as no part of the pig touched food or the mouth. Naturally the conditions in the factories did not allow for the ritual

washing of hands and face, one of the factors that often led to conflict between the workers trying to make a living and the rabbis

4. Gitelman, p. 20.

5. Pares, p. 381.

6. Mahler, p. 6.

7. Gitelman, p. 18.

8. Irving Howe, *World of Our Fathers* (New York: Simon & Schuster, 1983), p. 29.

9. Gitelman, p. 33.

10. A good summary of the eastern campaigns of World War I can be found in J.F.C. Fuller, *A Military History of the Western World*, Vol. 3 (New York: Funk & Wagnalls, 1954). This book also has a summary of the Polish-Soviet War of 1920.

11. S. Adler-Rudel, *Ostjuden in Deutschland 1880–1940* (Tüebingen: J.C.B. Mohr, 1959), p. 156.

12. Richard Pipes, *Russia under the Bolshevik Regime 1919–1924* (New York: Knopf, 1994, p. 109.

13. New York's Lower East Side has been extensively documented. For London, see David Englander, ed., *Documentary History of the Jewish Immigrants in Britain 1840–1920* (London: Leicester University Press, 1944). For Berlin, see Eike Geisel, *Im Scheunenviertel* (Berlin: Severin & Siedler, 1981). For the reaction of the Jews of the West to the coming of these ghettos to Western Europe and America see the next chapter of this book.

14. All figures for the number of immigrants necessarily must be approximate. Where records do exist, they list only the recorded immigrants, not those who slipped over the borders illegally.

15. I. V. Lenin, "The Attitude of the Worker's Party toward Religion," *Proleterii* No. 45, May 1909, reprinted in *Little Lenin Library* Vol. 7 (Bristol, England: n.d.), p. 16.

16. Leon Trotsky, *History of the Russian Revolution*, Vol. 3, trans. Max Eastman (New York: Simon & Schuster, 1934), p. 39.

17. The question of whether all Russians whose passports bear the notation "Jew" as nationality are Jews by Jewish religious laws

has troubled Orthodox communities in the United States, Germany, and Israel. For the first time, there are economic advantages to being classed as a Jew and there are at least some instances where such documentation has been purchased on the Russian black market. Being recognized as a Jew means easier immigration and refugee status as well as financial help from Jewish organizations.

18. Michael Cohn, *The Jews in Germany 1945–1993* (Westport, Conn.: Praeger, 1994), Chap. 8.

19. Ernst Klee, Willy Dressen, and Volker Riess, *Those Were the Days*, trans. Deborah Burnstone (London: Hamish Hamilton, 1988), pp. 23–37.

20. Lodz became Litzmannstadt on orders of the Führer Adolf Hitler on April 11, 1940.

21. Ignatz Bubis, *Ich Bin Ein Deutscher Staatsburger Jüdischen Glaubens* (Cologne: Kiepenheuer & Witsch, 1993), pp. 39–80.

22. Emmanuel Ringelblum, *Notes from the Warsaw Ghetto* (New York: Schocken Books, 1974).

23. For a full account of the organization and chain of command of the Nazi extermination campaign, see Reinhard Rurup, ed., *Topographie des Terrors* (Berlin: Willmuth Arenhovel, 1988).

24. D. Steven Spielberg (director), *Schindler's List*, available in both books and film, gives a good picture of such ghetto factories (Video LDMCA081629).

25. Klee, Dressen, and Riess, pp. 160–162.

26. Author's personal observation.

27. Ignatz Bubis, who heads the Central Committee of the Jews in Germany, is one. Jerzey Kanal, who heads the Berlin Jewish Community, is another.

28. *Nachrichten des Jüdischen Kulturverein Berlin*, Dec. 1995, p. 3.

3

The Migration of Ideas

The flood of refugees that came from Russia in 1880–1881 to the Austrian city of Brody was unwelcome to the Jews in the West. The Hebrew Immigrant Aid Society (HIAS) in New York threatened to have these refugees shipped back to Europe if they tried to come to the United States. Sir Julian Goldsmidt, representative of the London Mansion House Fund, wrote Baron Rothschild in Paris "that London could not receive any refugees from Brody." Joseph von Wertheimer wrote from Vienna "whether it was worthwhile to endanger the position of 1.5 million Jews in Austria-Hungary for the sake of the refugees from Brody." Dr. Hermann Makower of Berlin and Dr. Herman Bärwald of Frankfurt were especially hostile to the idea of admitting Eastern Jews into Germany.[1] Those were the reactions of the official representatives of Western Jewry to the Alliance Israelite Universelle, the Jewish umbrella organization founded in Paris in 1860. It was the beginning of a continuous debate that raged from 1880 to today about the admission of "foreigners" into the Jewish communities in the West. From 1880 on there would be hostility and social distance between the Eastern and Western Ashkenazi.

There was good reason for this panic on the part of the Western Jews who had just won at least some equality of status with the other residents of their countries. In Britain, Lionel Rothschild had finally been allowed to take his seat in the House of Commons in 1858 after having been rejected five times because he would not take an oath on his faith as a "Christian gentleman." Benjamin Disraeli, born a Jew although converted to Christianity at the age of thirteen, had become prime minister of England in 1874.[2] The Rabbis Adler, father and son, had managed to centralize British Jewish administration under the name United Synagogues and tried to get this institution equal status as the Church of England, the "established church."[3] They saw the foreign rabbis, especially the Hasidic rebbes, as a threat to their religious authority. The Anglo-Jewish establishment tried their best to get Eastern Jewish refugees to settle in the United States, Canada, or anywhere rather than have them settle in Britain. They were even ready to pay them to return to their homeland. This idea of getting rid of the refugees never worked, of course. About 100,000 Eastern Jews settled in England, outnumbering the 60,000 Jews that had been counted in England in 1880. Unable to gain acceptance, the Eastern Jews organized themselves into the Federation of Synagogues in 1887 and claimed equal authority over the Jews in Britain as the United Synagogues.[4] Rabbi Hermann Adler tried to obtain the help of Rabbi Yitzschak Etchanan Spector of Kovno, Lithuania, to help him fight this insurgence, to no avail.[5]

The arrival of a large number of workers willing to work for low wages roused anti-Semitic hostility both among the English workers and in the Houses of Parliament. Jews moving into inexpensive housing in Whitechapel and other areas of East London roused opposition in the local councils and residents. Having so many new tenants looking for lodging allowed the landlords to raise rents. Adding new elements into the cultural conservative pattern of these districts caused the older residents to complain about the habits and mannerisms of the newcomers. The fact that some of these new-comers were socialists who were willing to challenge the Chief Rabbi in front of his own synagogue didn't endear the newcomers either to the British Jewish establishment or to the London police.[6]

The situation in Germany was similar to that in Britain. Rosa Luxemburg, the leader of the *Spartakists* who came from Poland, wrote in 1894: "Who makes it to Berlin (from the East) is marked as a manipulator, a bringer of disease, panderer, smuggler and swindler."[7] The Jewish charitable organizations in Germany were always ready to help refugees when it was a matter of expediting emigration to America but were not inclined to help if the wanderer showed his intention to stay in Germany.[8]

The German Jews, even those from the former Polish provinces of Silesia and Pomerania, felt their fragile social and economic successes endangered. German Jews had built textile factories;[9] a Jew, Emil Rathenau, had created the German electrical industry; and there were Jewish bankers, like the Warburgs, the Mendel-sohns, and the Bodenheimers as well as the Rothschilds, who had become an international presence. As a symbol of the new Jewish self-confidence in Prussia, the Berlin Jewish community had built the 3,000-seat New Synagogue, whose opening was attended by Prinz Bismark, the prime minister.[10] To mark the "liberal" rather than orthodox ritual that was now followed in most German syna-gogues, this gold-domed edifice contained a magnificent organ.[11] The Westernized Jews of Berlin wanted as little as possible to do with the Eastern immigrants, not even with those Easterners like Chaim Weizmann, future president of Israel, who was studying at the university. Only a few Zionists and intellectuals had contacts in both groups.

Anti-Semitism did indeed follow the coming of the Eastern Jews to Germany, just as the German Jews had feared. In 1880 Jews were expelled from all student fraternities, which made the Jews into social pariahs in the German upper classes.[12] In 1885 all Russians, a group that included many Jews, were deported officially, but the actual immigration of Russian, Galician, and Romanian Jews into

Germany continued. As in Britain, the newcomers established a section in the eastern part of Berlin that came to resemble a Polish stetl. There was a strong Eastern Jewish presence in Saxony as well.[13]

The situation in the United States was no different than that in the Western European countries. Here, too, a social distance grew between the "German" Jews and the new arrivals from the East.[14] This social distinction was similar to the distinction that had existed between the Sephardic and German Jews. Many of the Jewish banking families, like the Lehmans, the Seligmans, and the Guggenheims, considered themselves to be more German than Jewish. Emphasis was on quiet wealth instead of showiness, except in the building of Moorish and Byzantine-style synagogues.[15]

Among the westernized and somewhat acculturated Jews, the mass immigration broke like a flood. The orthodox Eastern Jew, with his black coat and side curls, became the popular image of all Jews.[16] Newspapers found the Lower East Side to be good copy and showed its pushcarts and its poverty. The older Jewish population tried to claim that they were of different origin than these newcomers, but an examination of the family trees shows that this distinction is more sustainable in conversation than in fact. What is at issue is a class difference, not one of geographic origin.

Zionism was one of the ideas that helped blend eastern and western individuals into a joint movement. Its origins probably lie in the belief in a return to Zion found in many Jewish prayers. Perhaps it is best exemplified in the *Passover* service and the phrase "next year in Jerusalem" that is part of it.

When pogroms and other anti-Semitic actions in the late Victorian period all through Europe shattered the hope of assimilation and social acceptance by many Jews, the concept of a Jewish homeland, phrased in the form of nationalism current at the time among many different groups, began to gain some credence. Michael Hess of Bonn, Germany, demanded such a state in 1869 in his book *Rome and Jerusalem: The final Nationality Question.* In 1881 Leon Pinsker, a Jewish doctor in Odessa, published a pamphlet advocating such a state. Theodore Herzl, who had reported on the anti-Semitic Dreyfus affair for the Vienna *Freie Neue Presse*, came out with his seminal *The Jewish State* in 1869. His thesis combined the economic theories of Franz Oppenheimer on the need for owning land and the dignity of agricultural labor with the ideal of a return to Zion and the reestablishment of the Jewish people as a sovereign nation.

At the sixth Zionist congress in Basel, Switzerland, in 1903, the pressure of the idea of a return to Zion forced all the delegates, including Herzl, to abandon any idea of a temporary homeland for the Jews in Uganda or anywhere other than in Palestine.[17]

Zionism ran into considerable opposition among the Jews at first. Some rabbis saw Zionism as a tool of the assimilationists, while many intellectuals scoffed at the idea as being totally impractical in that it suggested moving sophisticated city dwellers into the primitive desert that Palestine was at the time. Many also objected to anything that would set the Jews further apart from their neighbors. They were also afraid that agitation would equate the concept of a Jewish national state with the propaganda that Jews were not patriotic and loyal to their state of residence.[18]

Gradually Zionism gained more acceptance, at least as an ideal, even if it was not something that was expected to be acted upon. Among the religious Jews in Poland and Russia, the *Mizrachi* and *Paola Zion* groups, which were both Zionist and religiously orthodox, were well established by 1906. Among the Western European romantics, Zionism gathered support because the Zionists, like the romantics, advocated return to the land and a simple life. Among the socialistically inclined, the idea of communal settlements run as cooperatives was appealing. Even some of the anti-Semites were for it. Emperor Wilhelm II of Germany granted Herzl favorable interviews while the emperor was visiting Constantinople and Jerusalem. The sultan of Turkey, Abdul Hamid, did not offer any overt opposition to Herzl's idea of trading the land of Palestine for the payment of the Turkish national debt. Even the anti-Semitic Russian minister of the interior, Count Plevne, listened to Herzl when he suggested that a Jewish homeland would relieve Russia of all of its revolutionaries.[19]

Two Jewish groups remained bitterly opposed to the concepts of Zionism. Among some of the very religious groups like the Satmar Hasidim, Zionism was a presumption because it proposed the rebuilding of Zion without the Messiah sent by the Deity as promised in the scriptures. The Jewish communists, such as Leon Trotsky, who witnessed the sixth Zionist congress as an observer-reporter, considered Jewish nationalism as a bourgeois step backward and a tool of Western capitalist imperialism.

The death of Herzl in 1904 at the early age of forty-four brought on a struggle for leadership of the Zionist movement.The group that now came to the fore was composed in large part of Russian Jews who had studied at the Humboldt University in Berlin. These included Chaim Weizmann, the first president of Israel, and Yitzhak Ben-Zvi, its second president. Many other leaders of the Zionists and Israel shared the same background.

The British government, looking for support among the Jews of the world and engaged in a war against Turkey, stated its support for the Zionist idea bluntly in the Balfour Declaration issued October 31, 1917. "His Majesty's government views with favor the establishment in Palestine of a national home for the Jewish people and will use its best endeavors to facilitate the achievement of this object."[20]

This declaration, of course, did not mean that all Jews would promptly pack their bags and emigrate to Israel. It did give a foundation of reality to the dreams of the Zionists. Now Zionism was a project in which nearly every Jew could participate without endangering his present home and status. The blue-and-white contribution boxes whose contents were used by the Jewish National Fund to acquire land in Palestine appeared in homes and stores of the Jews in Germany, Britain, America, Poland, and Lithuania. Only in the Soviet Union were they illegal. It became fashionable among many of the bourgeois Jewish families to mark joyous occasions or family events by planting trees in Palestine.

With the rise of Hitler, immigration to Palestine changed from an act of idealism to an act of desperation on the part of the Jews of Europe. By no means were all of the Jews who went to Palestine in the 1930s Zionists. Many of them settled in the European-style city of Tel Aviv instead of joining cooperative settlements or settling in the more traditional Jerusalem. As a result, although the German Jews became a sizable part of the population and a formidable economic force in Israel, they never rose to a position to challenge the leadership of Israel with the Jews of Eastern European origin.

Socialism rose to be a major factor in Jewish opinion at the same time as Zionism. The Bund, with its program of more rights for workers coupled with a demand for more social welfare, was founded in 1896. Its members were soon found spread through all of Poland and western Russia. Emigrants to the West took the program of Yiddish socialism with them to their new homes. In New York, the Workmen's Circle, with a similar program to that of the Bund, was founded in 1892. By 1910 it had about 39,000 members.[21] The Lower East Side elected a Socialist congressman, Meyer London, in 1914. The rise of the socialists in London was slower, but it was given a strong impetus by pacifist sentiment during World War I. In Germany the Social Democratic party gathered up most of the Jewish votes. In all of these countries, socialists and labor movements were closely bound together.

Socialism appealed to many Jews because of the similarity of the social program of these movements with the social program of the traditional kahillas. Both proceeded from the concept that the community is responsible for the needs of all its members and that the rich have an obligation to pay for the poor. Most kahillas supported their orphans, established schools, and helped students in institutions of higher learning. To aid the sick, to bury the dead, and to give financial assistance to those in need was not left to individual charity but to an organized social service to which the richer members of the community were pressured to contribute. The same pattern of organized social service also held for the

Landsmannschaften, the organizations of Jews who had emigrated from a particular town or region. These formed themselves into a benevolent society, sometimes with and often without forming a synagogue.

The socialists demanded the transfer of these functions from religious welfare societies to the government, which was thought to have greater financial resources and to be less tied to religious, regional, or personal biases. The socialists also had great appeal because they were organized on an international basis, so individuals moving from country to country found that they had a place where they could belong immediately. This was especially true of those who were no longer affiliated with any religious activity. Many others joined the socialists because they were on the side of the common people and the workers and against the establishment, Jewish and non-Jewish, which was conceived to be anti-immigrant and exploitive.

The needs of the new immigrants aroused an interest in new forms of social welfare on the part of the wealthier and more assimilated Jews of the West. Bertha Pappenheim, daughter of a Hungarian rabbi and patient of Siegmund Freud, organized the predominantly middle-class Jewish Women's League in Germany. This organization established homes and nurseries for unmarried mothers and their children and were prominent in the fight against "white slavery," the international trade in prostitutes.[22]

In New York the images of the reporter-photographer Jacob Riis brought the slums of the Lower East Side to the attention of all New Yorkers. In a report published in *Scribner's Magazine*, Spring 1892, he wrote:

> A population of over 111,000 inhabiting forty-five streets. All of them were foreigners, most of them Russian, Polish and Romanian Jews, and they are by all odds the hardest worked . . . of all our people. According to the records, scarce one third of the heads of families had become naturalized citizens, though the average of their stay in the United States

was between nine and ten years. The very language of our country was to them a strange tongue understood and spoken by only 15,837 of the fifty thousand and odd adults enumerated. Seven thousand of the rest spoke only German, five thousand Russian and over 20,000 could only make themselves understood to each other, never the world around them, in the strange jargon that passes for Hebrew on the East Side but is really a mixture of a dozen known dialects and tongues and some that were never known or heard anywhere else. In the census it is down for what it is—jargon, and nothing else. . . . Every synagogue, every tenement or dark back yard has its school and its schoolmaster, with his scourge to intercept those who might otherwise escape. . . . [T]he wise and patriotic men who are managing the Baron de Hirsch charity are making a useful handle by gathering the teachers in and setting them to learn English.[23]

This is the view of an outsider. Riis was a Dane and a Christian.

Even as these reports and pictures were published, conscientious leaders of the uptown Jewish community such as Isidor Strauss and Jacob Schiff had become aware of some of the problems of the new immigrants. These philanthropists established the Educational Alliance on the Lower East Side. At first this institution condescended to the Jews from the East and tried to get them to abandon their "medieval orthodoxy and anarchy," but later it became a real cultural center for Yiddish and for the Eastern Jews.[24]

Socialism also allowed women to rise to leadership on their own merits rather than as auxiliaries or heirs of their husbands or fathers. This, too, might be attributed in part to the independent role played by women in the ghettos, especially in economics. Rosa Luxemburg was one such socialist leader. She was born in Zamorsc, Poland, and went into exile in Geneva because of her left-wing activity. While in Switzerland, she helped found the Polish Social Democratic party in 1893. Five years later she was active in Prussian Silesia and then moved to Berlin. By 1914 she was coleader with Karl Liebknecht, a non-Jew, of the Spartakist, breaking with the Social Democrats over the issue of war credits in World War I. Although she preferred the weapons of the general strike over overt revolution, she became one of the leaders of the Spartakist uprising in Berlin in 1919. She was assassinated after the defeat of the revolutionaries by right-wing militarists, her body dumped into a canal. She has been a hero of the Left Wing ever since.

Esther Frumkin was another such woman leader. An extreme Yiddishist, she led part of the Bund into the Communist party in 1919. She was active in the campaign against Hebrew and the rabbis in Russia in the 1920s. She was accused of "nationalist bourgeois deviationism" by Stalin in 1937 and sent to a gulag with the other leaders of the Jewish committee of the Communist party.

Women also rose to become union leaders. Rose Schneiderman of the Accountants and Bookkeepers Union in New York played an independent role, as did some of the young female leaders of the textile unions.[25] Almost all of these women leaders were of Eastern European origin.

The whole concept of learning, always respected in Jewish culture, became interwoven with the new methods of achieving social action. An ever-increasing number of Russian Jews sought to study medicine instead of attending the traditional yeshivas. Since the number of Jews admitted to the Russian universities was severely restricted by quotas, many of these students went to universities in Austria and Germany, where they made up as much as 15 percent of the total student body. For women, the field of social work as a profession instead of merely charitable work opened up. These occupations became a source of pride by students and their relatives, especially among the more secular Jews.

In the West the study of law was also a matter of pride, since the law required both learning and dignity. In Eastern Europe and especially Russia, lawyers came out of a different tradition, that of *shadlan*, or intermediary between the Jewish community and the government. These intermediaries had to be skilled in using connections, flattery, and bribery, since Russian officials ruled as much by whim as by rigid application of the rules. When it was a matter of relief from taxes or obtaining a license or an exemption from military conscription, the shadlan often handled the matter.[26]

World War I shattered the unity of Zionism and Socialism as well as that of the Jewish world in general. Jew was set against Jew in a world at war. The *Jewish Chronicle* of London thundered in August 1914: "England has been all she could be to the Jews. The Jews will be all they can be to England."[27] In Berlin the *Allgemeine Jüdische Rundschau* trumpeted in turn: "The Jewish youth will volunteer for military service and the Jews of Germany will offer all their wealth and all their blood for the Fatherland."[28] The Social Democrats in the Reichstag, the German legislature, immediately joined their brethren on the conservative benches in voting for war credits, with the exception of the two Spartakists.

These patriotic appeals fell on somewhat deaf ears in England among the immigrants from the East. Many of them had fled the conscription of the tsar and the Austrian emperor. They had very little interest in aiding their oppressors who ruled Russia and felt they had little at stake in fighting Franz Joseph of Austria. In London the socialists organized protests attended by thousands against the British government proposal to draft immigrants under threat of immediate deportation to Russia. The protests became more virulent after the tsar was overthrown and the British government sent money, troops, and guns to aid the Whites, units that engaged in violent pogroms in the Ukraine and southern Russia. Despite this resistance, many Jews did serve in the armed forces of both Germany and the Allies.

After the war this service was a matter of pride to some Jews. In Germany the *Bund Jüdischer Frontkämpfer*, League of Jewish Front-line Fighters, was formed. Among other things, it tried to counteract right-wing propaganda about Jewish slackers and war profiteers.

For most Jews the disillusionment that set in after the end of the war meant a growth of those groups that had either opted for pacifism or actively resisted the war hysteria. Only the Zionists, who could point to the Balfour Declaration as a result of their help in the British war effort, were able to rebuild and strengthen their international organization. The Marxists, although gaining in absolute numbers, divided into violently hostile factions who fought out their disagreements with fists as well as words.

In Russia the Bolsheviks seized power in Moscow and St. Petersburg in October 1917, although they were not able to fully consolidate their power in all of Russia until 1923.[29] Almost immediately after seizing control, the Communists turned on the wealthy, including wealthy Jewish factory owners, merchants, and supporters of the old government. Those who could do so fled. Since there was no shelter for the Jews among the White counter-revolutionaries, these refugees went to the Western countries, primarily to Berlin.

In 1922 the Communists turned on their former allies, the members of the Socialist Revolutionary party, as well as on those intellectuals who did not slavishly follow the party line. At the same time, they intensified their antireligious campaign against priests, rabbis, and kahilla officials. Many of the victims of this first Communist purge who were tried by the revolutionary courts were sentenced to "external exile." Individuals in these groups and many others who were not actually put on trial fled westward, again primarily to Berlin, because it was accessible by rail and the anti-immigration laws blocked going to the United States.

Berlin became the center for Jewish intellectual life. Publishing in Yiddish and Hebrew flourished. These publications often found their customers in America and Eastern Europe, but printing costs in Berlin were low and authors and artists plentiful. Franz Kafka taught at a Jewish settlement house,[30] and Chagall and Lissitsky painted in Berlin, as did many other artists from the East. There were Yiddish playwrights and poets. There was even a small market for translations from Yiddish to German. However, economic conditions were hard, as runaway inflation ate up the gain from artistic productions. Gradually many of the painters and sculptors left Berlin for Paris. The Ecole de Paris included such Eastern Jews as

Chagall, Kisling, Pascin, Soutine, Jacques Lipshitz, and Chaim Gross. Many of these would emigrate once more from Paris to New York.

The political situation was not very favorable to immigrants from Russia, either. The Social Democratic government had allied itself with right-wing militarists to put down the left-wing uprisings in Berlin, Bavaria, and Thuringia. As a result of this alliance, Germany became more conservative. Many of the German Jews opted for bourgeois patriotism, and memorial tablets to "Our Heroic Dead of 1914–1918" were put up in many German synagogues. Deprived of the support of their fellow Jews, attacked as panderers and black marketers by an increasingly hostile press, the poor Jews of the Scheunenviertel faced ever more problems. Again and again the Prussian police raided this area looking for illegal aliens and smugglers. The massive raid of April 5, 1933, after the Nazi takeover, resulted in photographs and radio reports that showed the Jews as people in foreign dress speaking with Polish or Russian accents.[31] This material served the Nazi propaganda machine for many years, culminating in the notorious "Eternal Jew" exhibit in Munich in December 1937. The Jews of Leipzig, especially the Eastern Jewish fur workers, were subjected to the same treatment as their brethren in Berlin.[32]

In London anti-Jewish agitation was carried on as a campaign against "slackers and shirkers" as well as by classifying Eastern Jews as "Bolshevists and anarchists." The *Morning Post* and the *Evening News* printed a vicious series of attacks in March 1918.[33] These and attacks launched in the local borough councils against Jewish shopkeepers increased and resulted in the passage of the Alien Restriction Act of 1919 in the British Parliament. This act prohibited aliens from changing their names or serving in any civil service job and threatened immediate deportation for former enemy aliens. This kind of persecution gradually subsided over the years, and Eastern Jews were absorbed to a certain extent into the general body of British Jewry.

The biggest and most successful settlement of Eastern Jews in the West was in the Lower East Side of New York. Although anti-alien sentiment in the United States resulted in the restriction of immigration in 1921 and even more in 1924, the Yiddish community in New York showed a tremendous vitality. There were Yiddish newspapers, Yiddish theater, and Yiddish clubs ranging from extreme left-wing Marxist groups to the most orthodox religious study groups. This Eastern Jewish influence spread much beyond its geographic base. Jewish delicatessens featuring such Eastern dishes as pastrami, lox on a bagel, matzoh ball in chicken soup, and salami on Jewish rye could be found all over New York as well as in other cities. Jews, especially Eastern Jews, became dominant in certain economic fields, such as jewelry, scrap metal and metal finishing, entertainment, furs, and textiles.[34] Yiddish expressions drifted into American slang. The Eastern Jewish tradition of engaging in publicized charity brought a tremendous growth in donations to universities, hospitals, and settlement houses, both Jewish and non-Jewish. The pattern of public giving was adopted by the assimilated German Jewish families like the Lehmans and the Guggenheims, who now named wings of college buildings, museums, and social agencies after themselves. The Jewish practice of using social pressure to increase donations by publishing lists or inviting potential donors to group meals has been taken up by almost all American nonprofit organizations.

Gradually the Jews in America, Eastern and German, have become more integrated into American society and are divided today more by their religious orientation than by their geographic origins.

NOTES

1. Adler-Rudel, p. 7.
2. On a tour of the houses of Parliament in 1985, our guide pointed to a statue of Disraeli with the comment, "Our Jewish prime minister."
3. Englander, p. 34.
4. Ibid., p. 199.

5. Ibid., p. 204.

6. Ibid., p. 172.

7. Rosa Luxemburg, *Gesammelte Werke.* 6 Vols. (Berlin: Dietz, 1974–1979), Vol. 1, p. 20.

8. Adler-Rudel, p. 6.

9. For a full treatment of the role of the Jews in the textile industry, see Chapter 5.

10. Bilderarchiv Preussicher Kulturbesitz, p. 234.

11. The use of an organ in synagogue services was a subject of considerable debate between the orthodox Jews, who considered it an act of assimilation, and the liberals, who considered it permissible under Jewish law. See David Ellenson, "A Disputed Precedent: The Prague Organ in Nineteenth-Century Central European Legal Literature and Polemics," in *Leo Baeck Institute Yearbook 1995* (London: Secker & Warburg, 1995, Vol. 40, p. 251.

12. The statement read: "Every son of a Jewish mother . . . is by birth dishonorable and devoid of all nobler feelings. . . . He is morally degenerate. . . . As a Jew cannot be insulted, no Jew can demand satisfaction for insults suffered." Theodore Herzl, among many others, immediately resigned his membership in the fraternity Albia. Salamander, p. 274.

13. For a fuller description of the Jews in Leipzig, Saxony, see Chapter 4.

14. Steven Birmingham, *Our Crowd* (New York: Harper & Row, 1967), p. 6.

15. The Central Synagogue at Fifty-fifth Street and Lexington Avenue in New York City is one of many examples. It was built in 1872.

16. Even in 1980, I was told by my young students in Bedford-Stuyvesant in Brooklyn, "You don't look Jewish. You don't dress like them." The students were most familiar with the Lubavitcher Hasidim, whose headquarters was nearby.

17. The conflict within the Zionist movement is covered in Jehuda Reinharz, *Chaim Weizmann* (New York: Oxford University Press, 1985).

18. The "Protocols of the Elders of Zion," a polemic created by the tsarist police around 1905 and extensively reprinted in many places since, fantasizes about a plot by a central body of Jews to control the world. In another form, the same question of Jewish loyalty was behind the survey of Jewish soldiers conducted by the German General Staff in 1916.

19. *Spiegel Magazine Spezial 2/1992* (Hamburg), p. 92.

20. Englander, p. 305.

21. Howe, p. 357.

22. Marion A. Kaplan, *Die Jüdische Frauenbewegung in Deutschland* (Hamburg: Hans Christians Verlag, 1981), p. 228, states that Bertha Pappenheim's attacks against the role of the Eastern Jews in this "trade" was so violent that the Nazi rabble-rouser, Julius Streicher, republished them verbatim in his journal *Der Stürmer* thirty-two years later.

23. Jacob A. Riis, "Children of the Poor," *Scribner's Magazine*, May 1892, p. 542.

24. Howe, p. 230.

25. Ibid.

26. The Russian proverb runs, "God is in His heaven and the tsar is far away." In a land of poor communications, local officials were left much more flexible in using their discrimination in administering the law than was the case in countries of the West. Appeals from the decisions of the local Russian officials, while possible, were extremely complicated and expensive.

27. Englander, p. 313.

28. This editorial was published under a masthead that still carried the quote about the Jewish homeland in Palestine from the Zionist Basel program. Illustration in Bilderarchiv Preussicher Kulturbesitz, p. 347.

29. Kiev, the Crimea, and the central Ukraine did not fall to the Bolshevik armies until 1921. Siberia joined the Soviet Union in 1923. Poland, Estonia, Latvia, and Lithuania were able to keep their independence after bitter battles with local Bolshevists until

1939, and Finland, after defeating local uprisings, stayed independent, although it lost much territory to the Soviets.

30. Geisel, p. 48.

31. In 1933 the police were commanded by Hermann Goering in his capacity as Prussian interior minister, and the press was controlled by Joseph Goebbels, acting both as propaganda minister and Nazi party leader of Berlin.

32. Manfred Unger and Hubert Lang, *Juden in Leipzig* (Leipzig, 1988), p. 152.

33. Englander, p. 299.

34. The role of the Eastern Jews as furriers, entertainers, and in the textile trades will be explored in later chapters of this book.

4

The Fur Business

In 1554 the German merchants of the Hansa complained that the fur business was shifting from the Russian city of Novgorod to the Saxon city of Leipzig.[1] This shift continued until, between the years of 1860 and 1930, one third of the total fur trade in the world was carried on in a single street in Leipzig, the Brühl.[2] Most of this trade was in the hands of merchants who had come originally from Russia, Poland, or Galicia.

The attraction of Leipzig was its well-established semiannual fair, the *Messe*, as well as the central position of Leipzig between Eastern and Western Europe. For centuries Jewish traders brought big, heavily loaded wagons carrying bales of furs from Russia to be sold at the Messe.[3] The traders would start their trip in Russia, cross the frontier at the Galician city of Brody to minimize custom duties, and then head for Leipzig. Until 1832 no Jew was allowed to be a permanent resident in Leipzig, and burial for Jews dying in the city remained a problem. It was 1902 when the merchants of Brody finally got together to found the Brody Synagogue, which is still standing and in use.[4] However, the Saxon merchants were glad to allow the Jews to come to the city temporarily and set up their booths to buy and sell. Between 1688 and 1764, that is, a period of seventy-five years, the Leipzig city fathers registered 81,937 Jewish visitors to the Messe. Accurate records were kept since both their presence and their sales represented an opportunity to collect taxes and fees. At the Messe the Jewish merchants sold their furs and then used the money they had received to buy woolen cloth, ironwork, and other wares, which they sold in turn at the fair at Berditshew in the Ukraine.[5]

The wealth of furs coming into Leipzig from Russia was truly astonishing. Though there are no exact records in Leipzig, we can make a reasonable estimate from the size of the official tribute in furs extracted by the tsars from Siberia. In 1714 this official tribute amounted to 13,200 sable skins, 3,282 red foxes, 48 white foxes, and 259 sea otters.[6] The proportion of the furs of the various species was to change over the years, but the volume stayed quite constant. Siberian furs were supplemented by the skins of the animals hunted in European Russia, Finland, and Lithuania. Fur hunters are still operating in these areas today.

Sable, a forest weasel related to the American marten and fisher, was the undoubted king of the fur bearers.[7] Its fur is dense, warm, and light in weight, a coat of sable weighing only half as much as a coat of mink. The skin is strong enough to be easily sewn without tearing, much more so than squirrel skin. Since the animal is three times the size of a mink, fewer skins are needed to make a cloak. Its fur is of a rich brown color requiring no dyeing.[8] Occasionally a mutant black sable would be found in the traps, and cloaks of black sable skins were considered fit gifts for kings. Today, when wild sable has become scarce, its fur is still used for ceremonial dress among the tribes of Siberia.[9] In the 1930s a sable cloak would cost the equivalent of a year's wages of a worker. This made it well worth the effort to trap and transport the skins. Like all weasels, sable today is not trapped as often but obtained from animals raised in cages on a "fur farm."

When the Russian explorers and Cossacks reached the shores of the Pacific Ocean, the sea otter, a marine animal related to the weasels, was added to the list of favorite fur animals for the Russians. Its rich warm fur, also dark brown, competed with sable in price. A single sea otter skin would bring up to $200 in today's dollars. Again there was no limit to the greed of the hunters or to that of their employers, the Russian tsars. As an example of the number of animals killed, a ship belonging to the merchant Gregory Shelekov returned from a two-year stay at Kamshaka, on the shores of the North Pacific. It brought back a cargo of 2,000 beaver skins, 6,000 blue fox skins, 40,000 sea otter skins and 17 tons of walrus ivory.[10] There was profit to be made every step of the way: profit in granting the license to hunt, profit for the hunters, profit for the Russian middlemen, and profit for the Jewish traders bringing the furs to Western Europe. The sale of these masses of furs supplied the Russian rulers with funds and all the wealthier inhabitants of Europe with warm winter clothing. The trappers and entrepreneurs of Siberia usually brought their furs to the fairs at Nizhny-Novgorod (formerly Gorki) and Irbit in spring to be sold to the mostly Jewish traders, who handled transport and resale to Western Europe. Curing the skins was done mostly in Western European cities. A separate trade route went by way of Chinese merchants to Peking, a trade that still exists. The slowness of transport until the twentieth century, when railroads became more common in Russia, meant that it would be fall before the furs reached Leipzig or China.

From the 1550s to the 1850s, the Russians pushed their frontier steadily eastward, always pursuing the fur animals that brought them wealth. The development of the Siberian diamond mines and goldfields was almost a by-product of the fur trade. So was the collection of masses of fossil mammoth ivory and walrus teeth found at arctic beaches and river mouths.[11] To obtain furs the Russians endured the ferocious Siberian cold in winter and the clouds of insects in summer. They enslaved or destroyed tribes and nations from the Urals to Alaska. The exiles sent to Siberia grew food or built the fortresses that supported the fur trade. The excessive hunting decimated the game animals of each region in a relatively few years. Sable retreated to the deep woods, and the sea otter become almost extinct.[12] Other nations cared as little about animal preservation, as the record of seal hunting off Siberia and Alaska shows.[13]

The Jewish and Bokharan fur traders at the fairs in Nizhny-Novgorod were well aware of the decline of the quantities of sable, sea otter and beaver furs available to them. They had little control over the pattern of hunting and trapping, but survived in their business by increasing the trade in more plentiful furs such as Lithuanian hares, Mongolian marmot, and squirrel skins. They also dealt with the skins from renewable resources such as lambskins. These furs were obtained from the nomadic tribesmen of the dry interior of Central Asia. These lambskins became the karakul, broadtail and Persian lamb fur of commerce. The Turcomen and other tribesmen had to cull their herds to prevent overgrazing the limited pastures of the steppes. Lamb meat fed the nomads, and the next year the sheep bore a new crop of lambs. The finest furs came from unborn or newborn lambs, but all sheepskins were saleable. Dealers also bought goat and pony skins to be processed into the fine "Russian leather" that became the belts and purses for Victorian ladies.[14]

In 1892 the Emirate of Bokhara, today Uzbekistan, exported 700,000 skins of karakul, 800,000 white lambskins, 200,000 sheepskins, 20,000 gray lambskins, and 50,000 fox furs. The traders from Bokhara, many of them Sephardic Jews, carried them to the new railroad leading to Orenburg and Nizhny-Novgorod, where they sold them to the traders from Leipzig.[15]

To be a fur trader required becoming familiar with many tongues and many cultures and respecting them all without losing one's own culture and identity. This is a skill learned early by many Jews, who are so often a minority in a sea of strangers. Fur traders took long trips away from home, returning only for a short stay with their family and community. This meant that their wives had to learn to be independent and make their own decisions without waiting for the return of their far-travelling spouses. While many fur dealers were religiously orthodox at home, it would have been quite difficult for them to observe the full restrictions of religious law on their trips.

After 1870 the life of the Jewish fur traders became a little easier. Residence in Leipzig was now legal, and railroads made their trips shorter in duration and sometimes allowed the Russians to bring their furs to market in Leipzig instead of the buyers going out in the field. At the Leipzig fair of 1930, dealers from twenty-four countries exhibited skins taken from 3,000 species of animals. African leopards, South American chinchillas and nutria, Greenland foxes, European rabbits, and North American muskrats and raccoons were among the many kinds of animals that left their skins to be sold on the Brühl.

Machines changed the fur trade just like any other industry. The invention of the sewing machine and its improvements about 1870 allowed furs to be sewn into coats with sleeves instead of just being used for applied trim or wide cloaks suitable for women of all sizes.[16] At the same time, large cities with better transportation and better hotel accommodations began to take business away from Leipzig. In that town young boys steered buyers to boarding houses and apartments renting rooms, a practice that led to close social contacts within the industry, but gradually both buyers and sellers were demanding something more luxurious and more private than the accommodations Leipzig offered. World War I, political instability in Germany, and runaway inflation also helped to make Leipzig less desirable as the center of the fur trade.[17] The Holocaust eliminated the rest of the fur traders from Leipzig, although a few individual workers managed to survive by timely emigration or as slave laborers making fur clothing for the Wehrmacht out of seized or donated fur coats.[18]

London had always been the trading center for the furs gathered at the posts of the Hudson Bay Company in Canada. It had also handled the beaver furs imported from America, which were usually made into men's hats. When silk toppers replaced beaver hats, the furriers shifted products. Beaver was used for coat trim as well as material for full-length coats. London furriers also developed a process that turned sealskins into a lustrous black fur. It is London as much as any other city that created fur coats as high-fashion items as well as practical cold-weather wear.

By 1917 New York surpassed both Leipzig and London as a fur market. Part of this was due to the problems of World War I in Europe, but part of it was due to the utilization of American resources. From New York, fur buyers travelled to the swamps of Mississippi to purchase muskrat skins from the Cajun trappers and fishermen. In many of the small towns of the northern United States, Jewish merchants bought up the furs brought in by boys who ran a trap line on their farms in winter, both for extra income and to guard their chicken coops from four-footed predators like mink, fox, fishers, and skunks. Fur buyers from fashionable firms like Revillion Freres also travelled to the Arctic for the white fox skins made popular by Hollywood stars in the 1920s and 1930s.

Fur farms, places where animals were bred for their skins, also became common in America. Furs from these breeding factories competed with the wild furs of the trappers. The quality of the furs from the ranches might not be quite so high as that taken from wild animals, but the reliable supply and the lower price made up for that. It also allowed breeding of mutant animals like silver fox and platinum mink to order. Fur ranching, like fur trapping, was not in Jewish hands, but the buyers who purchased the furs were usually Jews.

Trading is, of course, only part of the fur business. Much needed to be done to the rough, dried skins before they were fit to cover the backs of fashionable ladies and keep them warm in the days before heated automobiles and covered shopping malls.

When the bales of furs arrived at the dealers, they were first sent for processing to the dyeing and dressing plants. This was a smelly process, and the plants working on skins and furs were usually located away from the centers of cities, where the odors might offend. For the New York market, A. Hollander & Sons built a plant in Newark, New Jersey, in 1890. By 1912 it employed as many as 700 workers, both men and women. In London tanning and dyeing were carried out in Bermondsey, east of the Tower, in what today is the Docklands district. While the trade has disappeared from there, the names of streets like Tanners and Morocco Street remind us of the former activities.

When the furs came back to the dealers from the processors, the sorters took over. They laid the skins next to each other for a match in color and pattern to make up "plates," a fur panel large enough for one side of the coat. This was a highly skilled trade that required the sorters to use their personal judgment. Most of the sorters were independent contractors rather than employees and specialized in one kind of fur. Sorters occasionally also dabbled in dealing with furs on the side.

Cutters then trimmed off paws and odd corners of the skins. These scraps were not wasted but assembled into caps and muffs. Sometimes they were even turned into plates of lower quality. This work with scraps required a great deal of sewing, work that was often performed by low-paid women workers who labored for contractors in small lofts or basements.

Fur workers and dealers were quite clannish, and much of the trade was broken into small units. There was the Mutual Protective Fur Manufacturers Association for dealers in medium- and low-grade furs and an Associated Fur Manufacturers group for those who dealt in top-quality skins.[19] The Fur Workers International Union had Branch Eight for Yiddish-speaking members and Branch Seventeen for Jews who spoke Russian. Fur processing in New York, which had been in the hands of Germans, became predominantly Jewish by 1892. Networks of dealers who came from one town or region in Eastern Europe helped each other and found jobs for sons or daughters of their friends and families. It was a trade that carried on many of the traditions of the stetl.

Working in the fur trade was unhealthy. The dust from the skins permeated the air and encouraged asthma, tuberculosis, and other lung ailments. Processing and dyeing used strong caustics and dyes, which ate into the skin and caused slow-healing sores. Some of the chemicals used were also strong carcinogens, although that was not understood at the time. However, by 1911 a New York State commission reported that eight out of ten fur workers suffered from occupational diseases.[20] While we have no comparable figures from London or Leipzig, the health situation must have been very similar to that in New York.

Unions in the fur industry, especially among the low-paid muff and cap makers, were formed early. By 1907 the workers were demanding pay for the Jewish New Year and the Day of Atonement from their bosses. Massive strikes occurred in the fur industry in 1912, 1914, and 1917. Overtime pay was one of the issues; the industry is strongly seasonal, and a fifty-four-hour work week during the busy season was considered nothing unusual. On the other hand, the workers were laid off as soon as slack times arrived. Among the Eastern Jewish immigrants, this was a formula for disaster, especially if illness struck during the season. Unions and fraternal orders had a strong attraction. Since many of the Eastern European workers had experience with Marxism at home, it is no surprise that fur workers' unions had strong ties to Marxist-oriented political parties and to the Workmen's Circle, with it socialist program.

Through the years the fur industry continued to display this mixture of strong individualism, tight regional and family networks, and union activity. Few young people who did not have relatives "in the business" could hope to succeed.[21]

The fashion designers who worked with the fur salons were not really considered part of the fur business but played a large role in it nonetheless. It was the designers who came up with boas, narrow fur scarves worn in the 1920s and 1930s. They also created the fashion of mutant minks and raccoon coats for men, a craze of the 1920s.

After World War II the fur trade declined, especially in the United States. Synthetics were discovered that would give nearly the same warmth as furs and were much cheaper. Population pressure caused a deterioration in the wild environment that sheltered the fur-bearing animals. The Holocaust decimated the skilled fur workers of Europe. In the United States the children of fur workers found more profitable occupational niches. Political instability in the fur exporting countries such as China and Iran made the trade more difficult. The cold war increased the duty charged on Russian furs, making fur coats even more expensive. For a time environmental groups created a climate that made wearing fur coats unfashionable or exposed the wearers in Western countries to outright physical attacks.

Things are changing again. The market for furs in Russia and China is increasing.[22] Fur-bearing animals are returning even to suburban areas, at least in the United States.[23] But the reviving fur trade is no longer a Jewish preserve. Indian merchants are peddling furs on the markets in Helsinki and Bergen, Norway as well as in the fur sales of New York. The oriental fur trade is firmly in the hands of the Chinese and Koreans. There are still some old Jewish firms in the New York fur district on 30th Street, but they are comprised of older men whose sons are in other professions.

NOTES

1. Joseph Schildhauer, *The Hansa*, trans. Katherine Vanovitch (Leipzig: Dorse Press, 1988), p. 234.

2. Klaus Metscher and Walter Fellmann, *Lipsia und Merkur* (Leipzig: Brockhaus Verlag, 1990), p. 87.

3. Leipziger Messeamt, *Georg Emanuel Opiz, Ein Zeichner der Leipziger Messe* (Leipzig: 1988).

4. The bigger Central Synagogue was opened in 1856 and burned by the Nazis in 1938. The Brody Synagogue, which follows the orthodox ritual, owes its survival to the fact that it is located in an apartment house and was therefore vandalized rather than burned by the Nazis.

5. Metscher and Fellmann, p. 96.

6. Yuri Semyonov, *The Conquest of Siberia*, trans. E. W. Dickes (London: Routledge & Sons, 1944), p. 136.

7. Sable, *martes zibbelina*, is a member of the family of animals that also includes the American marten and fisher. Sable is about 18 inches long plus tail.

8. The rich brown color of sable fur was also sought in other animals that became popular in the fur trade, i.e., sea otter, beaver, mink, and nutria, a South American river rodent.

9. Ludmilla Rastorgueva, *The Clothes of the North, National Dress of the Sakha Republic* (Yakut: 1994), #18.

10. Semyonov, p. 158.

11. Yakut Trade Mission, personal communication with author, 1993.

12. Today the sea otter is making a comeback off the coast of California under the strict protection of the federal Marine Mammal Act.

13. Rudyard Kipling, in his "Rhyme of the Three Sealers," wrote in 1893,

> but since our women must walk gay and money buys their gear
> The sealing boats they filch that way at hazard year by year.
> English they be and Japanee that hang on the Brown Bear's flank
> And some be Scot but the worst of the lot, and the boldest thieves
> be Yank!

Rudyard Kipling, *Rudyard Kipling's Verse 1885–1918* (New York: Doubleday Co., 1920), p. 129.

The Sea Wolf by Jack London (New York: Tor, 1995) also deals with ruthless poachers.

14. Today goat leather is usually sold as "genuine Morocco," but most often comes from Mali in West Africa.

15. Henry Landsdell, "Bokhara Revisited," *Scribner's Magazine* 11, January 1892, p. 58.

16. See illustration in this book from *Godey's Lady Magazine*, 1859.

17. The firm of Eitigon, one of the leaders in the Leipzig fur trade, is listed as a New York importer of Russian furs in *Fortune Magazine*, August 1932.

18. Heinz Muscat, personal communication with author.

19. Philip S. Foner, *The Fur and Leather Workers Union* (Newark, N.J.: Nordan Press, 1950), p. 46.

20. Ibid., p. 41.

21. Much of the information in this chapter comes from the author's relatives or their children "in the business."

22. *New York Times*, Oct. 12, 1995, p. 1.

23. The howls of wolves have been heard recently in St. Paul, Minnesota, beaver are becoming a nuisance by flooding roads with their dams in Minnesota and upper New York State, wild fisher are attacking domestic cats thirty miles north of Boston, and coyote have been accidentally killed within the borders of New York City.

Jewish House in Ushitza, Ukraine. Photo by Menachem Kipnis. Courtesy of YIVO Institute for Jewish Research.

Jewish Porters in Lublin, Poland, 1930. Siegmund P. Cohn Archives.

Religious School on Hester Street, New York. From Scribner's Magazine, May 1892.

Mt. Sinai Hospital, New York. From Manual of the City of New York, 1869.

Rosa Luxemburg as Communist Labor Leader. Postage Stamp of East Germany, 1955.

Sewing Woman's Home, New York, 1891. From Darkness to Daylight by Mrs.
Helen Campbell.

Cigarette Making in London. From Squire Magazine, 1902. Photo provided by Mary Evans Picture Library, London.

"Russian" Cloak of Velvet and Sable with Silk Lining. From Godey's Ladies Book, 1859.

Fur Workshop in Leipzig, Germany, circa 1936. Courtesy of Edgar J. Malecki.

Jewish Owned Men's Clothing Store, Loudonville, Ohio, 1917. Strauss Family Archives.

Advertisement for Dance Halls, Cleveland, Ohio, 1913. Rosenthal Family Archives.

Performance of the Opera "Queen of Sheba" at Rabbi Ephraim Carlebach School, Leipzig, Germany, 1937. Courtesy of Edgar J. Malecki.

"Koschre Tanz" at Modern U.S. Wedding. Courtesy of Mr. and Mrs. Charles Merber.

Angels #2. Watercolor by Edouard S. Belyat. Courtesy of Yeshiva University Museum.

5

Cloth and Clothing

Many strands of long-term Jewish economic activities contributed to the large role played by Jews in the clothing and textile industries. For hundreds of years, Jewish peddlers had been buying handwoven cloth, duck and goose feathers, as well as other agricultural products from the peasants in the German borderlands in exchange for salt, sugar, tea, ironwork, pots, and notions. In 1764 Rabbi Fraenkel, chief rabbi of the province of Silesia, obtained a license giving him and his descendants unlimited trading rights in the province. This was in line with Frederick the Great's policy to expand Prussia's trade with the East by using Jewish connections that already existed. Gradually the house of Fraenkel as well as the firm of Meyer Kauffmann and others became specialized textile wholesalers.[1] To ensure a good supply of cloth, these entrepreneurs lent money to the peasants to purchase or build hand looms. The woven linens were brought to the entrepreneur's factory for dyeing, bleaching, and finishing. The finished cloth would then be taken to the Messe in Leipzig or Frankfurt on the Oder for sale, for either domestic use or export.

The Industrial Revolution that had begun in England in the eighteenth century made serious inroads in this trade. By 1800 British mills were equipped with steam- or water-driven spinning and weaving machinery. Linen cloth was being replaced by cotton made available by the invention of the cotton gin in America. Cotton thread is easier to spin and weave than the harder linen. By the 1830s, British cloth from Manchester was on sale in Leipzig, and the watercolorist Opiz sketched Bokharan and Russian Jewish merchants buying this cloth from Jewish sellers. The head coverings leave no question about the religion of both buyers and sellers. The Silesian merchants tried to compete by distributing cotton thread to their weavers[2] and later by reducing the price paid for handwoven cloth to starvation levels. This ruthless wage cut provoked a minor revolt of the weavers in the Bohemian mountains, but the revolt was promptly suppressed by the Prussian military. There were twelve dead and twenty wounded, including both striking weavers and innocent bystanders. This heavy-handed action brought intense criticism of the government by the German liberals. The socialist newspaper *Vorwärts*, which counted Karl Marx and Friedrich Engels among its correspondents, wrote about the weavers' revolt as part of its campaign against the excesses of the new capitalism. Fifty years later, Max Pincus, a member of the Fraenkel textile family, furnished some technical details of these consequences of the changeover from hand weaving to factory work to the dramatist Gerhart Hauptmann, and this author fashioned the information into the powerful play *The Weavers*.[3] The play, in turn, inspired the German artist Kaethe Kollwitz to create her world-famous lithographs on the topic; these have been reproduced frequently and have helped to give the textile industry the bad reputation that has persisted until today. In England there was a similar uprising of hand weavers who called themselves the Luddites and smashed machinery in some of the British factories. The Kollwitz lithographs and the similarly powerful photographs by the American Lewis Hine overshadow the fact that children were equally exploited by the glass and iron factories.[4]

The Jewish factory owners of Silesia abandoned handwoven production and bought British weaving machinery at the World's Fair in London in 1851. They then proceeded to build factories that centralized cloth production, some of these factories employing as many as 4,000 people. Cloth factories rose not only in Silesia but also in southern Germany; Austria; Poland, especially in Lodz; and in St. Petersburg, Russia. Some of these new factories were daughter corporations of the firms of Kauffmann and Fraenkel. Factories on this scale and the employees they drew destroyed a large part of the old village life, both Jewish and non-Jewish. Rosa Luxemburg wrote about the textile industry and the new Jewish proletariat in her Ph.D. thesis in Zurich in 1897.[5] In her thesis she also attacked the Jewish capitalists who were using the profits acquired from their textile operations to expand into Polish coal mining and large-scale farming. In Silesia, Jewish firms entered the coal and iron industries, furnished rails for Russia, and produced chemicals.[6] The base for these industrial enterprises lay in the money deposited in private Jewish banks in Breslau (Wroclaw) by the textile entrepreneurs.

At the same time that some Jewish firms were building up their textile kingdom, many Jewish peddlers began to settle down in the small towns along the railway lines and the improved roads. Here they opened stores that sold yard goods and, when sewing machines made ready-made clothing available, sold this as well. A network of Jewish travelling salesmen connected these Jewish storekeepers with the manufacturers.

In the United States, a pattern similar to that in Poland developed, the store owners of German or Eastern Jewish origin often being the only Jewish family in town.[7] In some cases these small stores would develop into department stores, in other cases, into specialized clothing factories,[8] but in most cases they remained small-scale retail operations.

In Britain immigrant Jewish peddlers had dominated the old clothes trade in early Victorian times. By 1851 many of these peddlers had shifted to storekeeping as the availability of ready-made clothing cut into the secondhand clothing market.[9]

In the late nineteenth century a flood of Eastern Jews fleeing economic and political repression in Galicia and Poland appeared in London, Berlin, and Vienna. Members of the same group also came to New York. Some of these new immigrants were skilled tailors and dressmakers who began to open small dressmaking establishments or went to work in the larger tailoring shops.

An ever-expanding market for textiles and clothing was created by the new, large-scale department stores in big cities. Many of these were owned by German Jews. In the United States the Lazarus family (Federated Stores), the Strauss family (R. H. Macy, Abraham & Strauss), Neimann-Marcus, and Gimbels represented these merchant princes. In Germany it was the Tietz, Israel, Wertheim, and Schocken department stores that were Jewish owned. Montgomery Ward and Wanamakers were some of the non-Jewish stores. All of these department stores maintained profitable yard goods, clothing, and notions departments that sold not only to the customers visiting the store but also to others by mail order.[10] Department stores and mail-order houses also supplied the dressmakers and tailors who travelled from house to house, making clothes to measure, and those thrifty housewives who sewed clothing for their families.[11] Only gradually did ready-made clothing replace made-to-order dresses and suits, as visits to stores became easier with the advent of the automobile.

A perusal of the Sears and Roebuck catalogue of 1897 gives an idea of the range of textile products available to the average consumer before the automobile.[12] Silks came from Lyons, France, as well as from China and Japan. This was one of the few branches of the textile trade not in Jewish hands but rather controlled by the "old China hands" of New England who had traded with China since 1800. Yard goods were advertised as coming from Silesia, England, and the United States, which produced Kentucky jeans. Laces came from Madeira, Italy, and Germany. There were ribbons, beads, and trimmings from many places around the globe. Ostrich feathers from South Africa were advertised, but not bird-of-paradise feathers from Indonesia nor egret plumes from Florida. Whether this was a matter of cost or a response to the movement to protect the birds that was under way at the time is not known. However, the feather and notion buyers were also often Eastern Jews, sometimes the same buyers who bought skins in winter.

Many of the department store owners saw themselves as liberals in the way they treated their employees. Schocken, in Germany, for instance, maintained a vacation home for employees and furnished free milk to undernourished apprentices and "cash boys."[13] Macy's and Gimbels established pensions and a credit union quite early, and Benjamin Altman left his whole store to a foundation for the benefit of his employees. Of course, this liberal attitude did not extend to allowing unions for employees nor a restriction on employing children as long as this was legal. It was a paternal liberalism that was practiced, not a democracy, and employees who patronized a restaurant designed for their "betters" or who failed to follow the social rules established by the bosses were soon fired.[14]

Buyers in department stores were given a great deal of freedom in running their department as long as they showed an adequate profit. Many of these buyers were as widely travelled as the fur buyers and, like them, were not quite considered ladies and gentlemen in the Victorian social scale. This social distinction worked to the advantage of Jews, who, not being Christians, were barred from the social status of "gentleman" in any case. Drummers, that is, travelling salesmen, usually stayed in commercial hotels near the railway station rather than the fancier establishments patronized by the upper class. Some hotels made no secret of the fact that they did not cater to "Hebrews," no matter how rich.[15]

Each department store maintained a tailoring department for special orders and alterations. This was usually manned by skilled tailors and dressmakers from Eastern Europe. However, the bulk of ready-made clothing was produced by outside contractors. This contracting created a tremendous home industry, although basements and small lofts were also utilized for it. Department store cutters sliced out the needed material for dresses or coats on order, added buttons and notions to the pile, and handed all of this over to a contractor or a middleman. The contractor in turn distributed the goods to smaller workshops or to home workers. Because of the difficulty of transporting the bundles of goods without loss or damage from weather, the small workshops were usually located in tenements in poorer areas close by.[16]

Pay for sewing was on a piecework basis, and this system soon gave rise to the term "sweatshop" or "sweated industry." All the family would help make a living, including the women and children, since the pay earned by the entire family was usually just above the absolute minimum needed for existence. A bad season, illness, or blacklisting by a contractor meant absolute misery. There was no such thing as health insurance, unemployment insurance, or working hours. The economic reasons for the existence of the sweatshops were spelled out perfectly by Anil Nayar, who operated a small wholesale operation, although she spoke of today rather than the turn of the century.[17]

She pointed out that it is relatively easy to enter the field of clothing production because it requires little capital. However, this very lack of capital reserves exposes the entrepreneur to the threat of cancellation by the buyers, a threat that the buyers are all too ready to use to force down prices. Since the entrepreneur is helpless because of the small size of his plant to force down prices of the raw material in turn, he attacks the only costs he does control, the price of labor. Either wages are cut or the demands for production are increased by a speedup.

Any attempt by workers to organize for higher wages or better working conditions is resisted by both the entrepreneurs and the buyers, since any increase in labor costs would jeopardize their profit margins. Since textile production is labor-intensive, buyers are constantly on the search for environments with lower labor costs.

This exploitive system aroused the attention of social reformers, especially in England and America. One of them, Mrs. Helen Campbell, has left us an excellent description of the tenement home-workshops. Her description deals with New York but would apply equally well to Whitechapel or Spitalfield in London, to Lodz in Poland, or to the Scheunenviertel in Berlin.

"In a small room in Hester Street a woman was at work on overalls. . . . Mame [her daughter; the name was changed] has learned to sew on buttons first rate and Jinny does almost as well. Mame is seven and Jinny is going on six. In the next room a Jewish tailor sat at work on a coat and by him a child of five was picking threads from another coat." Mrs. Campbell also describes the role of the middleman as she saw it. "For such work a sewing machine must be owned and as getting one even on the installment plan is often quite beyond the worker, this fact is taken advantage of by a number of 'sweaters' who rent basements and act as middlemen, taking work in great packages from the cutter of the manufacturing house and paying the women so much per dozen for the work done. . . . But every order of work goes on also in the tenement houses where women who own a machine can do work."[18]

Gradually work shifted from the homes and basements to larger workshops, where the concentration of a larger number of workers made for a more efficient system in terms of distribution of goods and quality control. These workshops were found, for the most part, within walking distance of the tenements. Attempts to regulate such workshops by the passage of laws was evaded both by employers and employees. Everyone considered the government inspectors to be enemies, not protectors. A London inspector of 1905 reported to a parliamentary committee that in a typical plant he found that no overtime records had been kept and presumably no overtime paid. There was inadequate time given for meals. There were underage employees, and there were numerous other violations of health and labor laws. At the time he was at the plant, workers pretended to be members of the family and thus exempt from labor laws, while others hid in the toilets, obviously cooperating with the Jewish owners' attempts to evade the law.[19]

In America and England, work conditions in the sweatshops and textile factories gave rise to a militant labor movement, Jewish led, as were the employee associations. Government legislation was believed to lead only to bureaucratic corruption by both sides. In Germany the fact that dress shop workers were mostly Eastern European Jews led the German Social Democratic unions to largely ignore this field in favor of concentrating on organizing heavy industry and mining workers.[20] In Poland, the Lodz textile workers went on strike as early as 1893. In New York the most famous labor action among the Jewish workers was the shirtwaist (blouse) laborers' strike of 1910. This strike, like many others, was instigated by teenage girls acting against the advice of the more cautious labor leaders. At a mass meeting held at Cooper Union Hall on November 11, 1910, the main featured speakers were officials such as Samuel Gompers, former cigar worker and now head of the American Federation of Labor, and Meyer London, the socialist congressman from the Lower East Side. Finally Clara Lemlich, a teenage textile worker, obtained the floor. "I am tired of listening to speakers who talk in generalities," she shouted in Yiddish, "What we are here for is to decide whether or not to strike. I offer a resolution that a general strike [of the industry] be called now."[21] Local 25 of the International Ladies Garment Workers' Union had reasons for advising caution. They had a paid-up membership of slightly more than one hundred and only four dollars in their treasury. But teenage enthusiasm carried the day. Despite the thugs who beat up pickets regardless of age and sex, and strike breakers hired by the Eastern Jewish bosses, the four-month strike made important gains for the labor movement. However, most important, it gave young, unmarried women a status in the Jewish community and a sense of their own importance. Their elders might consider them *verrückt*, crazy, but they respected the workers' devotion to their cause. The young Jewish women also gained a sense of solidarity with their Italian fellow workers with whom they had shared the picket lines. At the same time, these labor disputes set Jew against Jew and destroyed some of the sense of Jewish unity that had held the ghetto community together. What prevented a total shattering of the sense of community was the generally acknowledged fact that anti-Semitism and anti-Jewish discrimination remained a reality in daily life, regardless of political divisions or class status. Jew might fight Jew, but against outsiders the Jewish ranks closed.[22]

The sweatshops came to national American consciousness through the tragic Triangle Shirtwaist Company fire of March 25, 1911. As was customary in these sewing shops, there were many loose scraps of cloth lying on the wooden floor, a fire hazard. The doors to the staircase were locked to prevent workers from smuggling out goods. When fire broke out, only a few workers were able to escape by way of the stairs by the time the doors had been smashed open. Many of the rest were driven by the flames to the window ledges on the eighth, ninth, and tenth floors. The firemen were helpless, since their ladders reached only to the sixth floor and their safety nets could not hold the bodies of those who jumped. For eighteen minutes, hundreds of horrified onlookers watched girl after girl launch herself into the air to her death. When it was all over, 125 girls between the ages of 18 and 25 were dead. For days the national press and the Yiddish *Daily Forward* carried pictures and articles about the victims. Uptown German Jewish rabbis as well as leaders of the Lower East Side community voiced elegies. There were investigations and hearings. Social reformers like Frances Perkins, later the first secretary of labor under President Franklin D. Roosevelt, and labor leaders like David Dubinsky of the Amalgamated Clothing Workers were energized. But the building from which Frances Perkins saw the workers jump still stands,[23] and so do the sweatshops that exploit immigrants. In 1987 a German refugee from Hitler recalled her first job in the United States, in a corset factory where she worked on a sewing machine and learned English "from a bunch of Italian ladies."[24] In 1960 the author still carried bundles of dresses from the steaming lofts of contractors where they had been sewn together to the fashionable dress shops on Madison Avenue.

Today in the United States, the sweatshops employ mostly Latino or Oriental immigrant labor under conditions not much better than those of 1890, but much of the textile trade has been internationalized. Sweatshops in Thailand and Guatemala, in Bulgaria and China, as well as in many other countries produce the blouses, sweaters, and suits that are sold in the boutiques of New York, Paris, London, and Milan.

The home workshops did offer something of value to the Eastern Jewish immigrants besides a starvation wage. Perhaps some of the hidden benefits can be seen when we examine the trade in home-rolled cigarettes. This was an occupation created by immigrants from Poland and Galicia who settled in London, Dresden and Berlin between 1870 and 1910.

Like textiles, cigarettes were produced in the home and required almost no start-up capital. Unlike the clothing trade, cigarette production had no contractors and no middlemen. Tobacco for 95 pfennigs and cigarette paper for 20 pfennigs were sufficient to produce a thousand cigarettes. A family blessed with several older children to help could produce 3,000 cigarettes a day. The cigarettes were then peddled on the streets and in restaurants and sold to local tobacco stores by young women and boys. Clever cigarette rollers had their own brand name imprinted on the cigarette paper and then sent their friends to create a demand for that "brand." This trade was finally destroyed when cigarette-making machinery began to drive out the hand-rolled product, in about 1906.[25] It is important to remember that such a home industry existed and the reasons for it. Home work, even under harsh conditions and low pay, was preferred among Jews to domestic service or far-away factory jobs. A woman working at or near her home could care for her young children, cook a meal for her husband, or even keep the children near her while she worked, and her children were often gainfully employed after they reached the age of six. No one bothered to check immigration or employment papers, and there was no need to learn the language of the country. Religious restrictions regarding food or the Sabbath could be observed. There was no need to have a long, formal apprentice period or to deal with government bureaucracy about licenses.[26]

Many home industries flourished in addition to textile and cigarette work. Matchbox making, ornamental flower making and feather stripping were all primarily home industries. The textile industry simply utilized a system already in existence. Low rates of pay and unhealthy working conditions existed in almost all home industries and in small workshops.

However, the textile industry at least offered a chance for advancement. This was something not offered in other home workshop fields. With luck or help from a relative or an outside loan, the individual could acquire one or even two sewing machines and so advance into the ranks of middlemen or contractors. A clever boy could be taken on as an apprentice cutter or a clever girl could rise to become a designer or even a buyer. It didn't happen very often, but the dream of social and economic rise, like the dream of winning in the lottery, was in the range of possibilities.

The image of the textile industry, especially the dress- and suit-making industry, has stamped the image of the Eastern Jew living in the West. If he is successful, he is usually pictured as a fast-talking "boss" of a small shop sitting at his desk in shirtsleeves or walking among the sewing machines rather than as an executive in a fancy office. He is always pictured hunting for a "deal" that would improve his razor-thin margin of profit. He would take advantage of his female employees in a financial sense but very rarely in a sexual sense. The fact that his wife or some other relative would very likely be his bookkeeper precluded this. Outside of his business, he would be ready to contribute to charity and would respect learning of all kinds, though he himself was not highly educated. His English or German would be accented and his expressions pungent.

A good season in the textile trade could also produce a small surplus of funds for the family. From this surplus, small as it might be, money could be sent back to support parents in the old country or to pay the fare of another member of the family emigrating to America. There were Jewish banks on the East Side and the "ghetto bank" in Whitechapel, London, which remitted nearly one million rubles to Poland and Russia. Remittances as small as five rubles were available.[27] These small sums squeezed out of the miserable pay or profits often meant the difference between eating or starving in the ghettos of Russia and would keep up the contact between those who had emigrated and the folks at home. In some cases, however, the contact was broken, and the immigrant would start a new family in his new home, abandoning fiancée or wife and children in the old stetl.

Today many of the large textile firms are international corporations. Quite a few are still Jewish owned, such as Limited or Barney's, based in New York. Others have Sephardic Jews as owners, such as the Strawberry, Conway's, and Farah's firms. Still others are firmly international, such as Benetton or Stephanel. However, a good bit of the old images still linger, though the reality that inspired the image has long dissipated, as has the cigar smoke. The heritage is still strong, though, and the term sweatshop is usually applied to textile sewing shops in any country.

NOTES

1. Konrad Fuchs, "Jüdisches Unternehmen in Schlesien," in *Menorah* eds. Julius H. Schoeps, Karl E. Grözinger, Ludger Heidi, and Gert Mattenklett (Munich: R. Piper, 1994), p. 71.

2. Max Pincus, "Der Aufstieg der Firma S. Fraenkel 1827–1900," ms. in Leo Baeck Institute, New York.

3. For a full discussion of the revolt and the political and artistic consequences seen from a Marxist standpoint, see Wolfgang Buettner, *Weberaufstand im Eulengebirge 1844* (Berlin: Deutscher Verlag der Wissenschaften DDR, 1982).

4. John Spargo, *The Bitter Cry of Children* (New York: Grosset & Dunlap, 1906), p. 212, gives a list of 213 children employed:

34 Boys are glass factory workers (These are mostly Slavs & Italians)
23 Boys and 57 girls are textile workers
33 Boys and 22 girls are employed in the tobacco industry
18 Boys and 26 girls are in rubber factories, wire factories or work in candy factories

5. Rosa Luxemburg, Vol. 1.

6. Fuchs, p. 81.

7. The author has personal acquaintance with such Jewish families in Loudenville, Ohio, South Hill, Va., and Gloucester, Mass.

8. The Mighty Mac outdoor clothing factory of Gloucester, Mass., developed out of a firm peddling outdoor clothing to fishermen sailing on schooners. It has since been sold to a Korean firm, and the plant in Massachusetts was closed. Levi Strauss began as a peddler turning tent material into work clothing in California.

9. Henry Mayhew, *London Labor and London Poor*, ed. Peter Quennell in one volume (London: Spring Books, n.d.), p. 207. Original edition published in 1851.

10. *Bloomingdale Catalog 1886* (Reprint, New York: Dover, 1988).

11. Clothing was home sewn until the 1930s, especially in localities such as the hill country of the Appalachians and the Great Plains.

12. *Sears Roebuck Catalogue 1897* (Reprint, ed. Fred L. Israel, New York, Chelsea Publications, 1968).

13. Gesellschaft fur christlich-jüdische Zusammenarbeit, *Juden in Sachsen* (Leipzig: Evangelische Verlagsanstalt, 1994), p. 39.

14. Uwe Westphal, *Berliner Konfektion und Mode*, 2nd ed. (Berlin: Edition Hentrich, 1988), p. 33.

15. Birmingham, p. 149.

16. Berlin's Scheunenviertel, New York's Lower East Side, and London's Whitechapel are examples of such locations.

17. Anil Nayar, Letter to the Editor, *New York Times*, October 21, 1995.

18. Helen Campbell, *Darkness and Daylight* (Hartford: A.D. Worthington, 1891), p. 145.

19. Englander, p. 58.

20. Uwe Westphal, personal communication with author.

21. Howe, p. 298.

22. The assassination of Prime Minister Rabin of Israel was so shocking to the Jewish community because it was carried out by a Jew against a Jew.

23. Ronald Sanders, *The Downtown Jews* (New York: Dover, 1987), p. 393.

24. Michael Cohn, *From Germany to Washington Heights* (New York: Yeshiva University Museum, 1987), Interview #17.

25. Scheiger, p. 426.

26. Some of the same advantages of working at home can be seen today among the many who use their computers to do their work at home rather than going to the office. The fact that the companies save money on office rent also helps, of course.

27. Englander, p. 58.

6

The Music Makers

In the latter part of the nineteenth and early twentieth centuries, Jewish virtuosos from Eastern Europe flooded the field of classical music. Among them were the pianists Vladimir Horowitz and Arthur Rubinstein; the violinists Mischa Elman, Jascha Heifetz, and Ephraim Zimbalist; the cellists Emanuel Feuerman and Gregor Piatagorsky; as well as double bass players like Serge Koussevitzky, who later switched to conducting. The list could be extended almost indefinitely. There were Jewish conductors, singers, and composers as well. The ones listed here were all of Russian origin, but there were also many Jewish musicians from Hungary, Germany, and even the United States. Such Americans as Jan Peerce, Yehudi Menuhin, and Leonard Bernstein were of Eastern European origin. The dominance of Russian Jews was very noticeable. Nor has the flood of Jewish musicians from Russia abated. Twelve thousand Jews who emigrated to Israel from Russia since 1989 have listed themselves as professional musicians.[1] Many other Russian musicians emigrated directly to the United States or to Germany.

Such outpouring of Jewish musicians from the East cannot be attributed simply to talent. There must be both an economic and a cultural base for the musicians. There must be social approval for music and musicians in both the Jewish and the non-Jewish communities. There have to be sufficient opportunities for professional training and at least the possibility of making a decent living by playing classical music. Such a system must exist not only for the genius virtuoso but also for the many competent musicians who furnish the players for orchestras and become the less well known soloists. In addition, it must be possible both politically and socially for Jews to enter the profession. This last was a problem in many professions at the turn of the century, when there were strong anti-Semitic and antiforeign feelings in the countries of Western Europe.[2]

Both Richard Wagner and Franz Liszt complained in print about the number of Jewish musicians in the 1850s and 1860s.[3] Joseph Joachim was the kind of Jewish musician who aroused their professional jealousy. Like so many musicians, he was an internationalist, appearing on the stage in many countries. He was born in Hungary in 1831. He performed with Clara and Robert Schumann. The tsar of Russia gave him a free pass for all Russian railroads. In Berlin Joachim directed the musical academy from 1868. Like so many of the violin virtuosos of the period, Joseph Joachim was a child prodigy. He performed at the Leipzig Gewandhaus at the age of thirteen. He had been a student of Mendelssohn, who was Gewandhaus conductor at the time.

Both Mendelssohn and Joachim allowed themselves to be baptized as a means of furthering their careers, but neither lost their interest in furthering the progress of young Jewish musicians. Among those whom Joachim encouraged was the young Vladimir Horowitz. This networking among Jewish performers, teachers, and agents was to characterize the field until today.

Leopold Auer (1845–1930) was another Hungarian Jew who was both a well-known performer and a teacher of Russian violinists. In Odessa and St. Petersburg, where he was professor of violin between 1886 and 1917, he taught Mischa Elman, Jascha Heifetz,

Nathan Milstein, and Ephraim Zimbalist, among others. An idea of Auer's qualities as a performer can be gained by the fact that Tchaikovsky dedicated his violin concerto to him. Not all of the Russian composers were so friendly to Jews. Mikhail Glinka, Mily Balakirev, and Modest Mussorgsky all attacked the "Jewish musicians."[4] At a different time and place, Virgil Thompson, the American composer, was to complain about "a Jewish mafia that passed jobs around among themselves."[5] Leopold Auer, like Mendelssohn and Joachim, allowed himself to be baptized but fought with the Russian authorities in St. Petersburg for permission for the Jewish families of his Jewish pupils to stay in St. Petersburg, that is, outside the Pale of Settlement.[6]

Even more influential as teachers were the brothers Anton and Nikolas Rubinstein, no relations to the later pianist Arthur Rubinstein. Nikolas was the head of the Moscow Conservatory and founder of the Russian Musical Society. His brother Anton was a composer and founder of the St. Petersburg Conservatory. It seems impossible to read anything about Russian music of the period without coming across a mention of these two teachers and their influence.

The young music students of the turn of the century were not rebels against the values of their parents. They were, instead, part of the bourgeois Jewish tradition of the time, which made music a part of everybody's education and civilized living. Vladimir Horowitz's mother had studied piano at the Royal Kiev Music School. His uncle was the head of the music school at Kharkov and had studied under the composer Scriabin at the Moscow Conservatory. Vladimir's older sister played piano and was originally considered the musical genius of the family. Both of his brothers were considered competent if not inspired musicians.[7]

Arthur Rubinstein's background was also middle-class Jewish, and he was sent from Lodz, Poland, to his godmother in Berlin to further his musical studies.[8]

"Berlin was the musical center of the civilized world, its prestige founded on the music of the past and flourishing still in great orchestras and conductors, not to mention the most informed audiences to be found anywhere," wrote Yehudi Menuhin.[9] A concert in Berlin or elsewhere in Germany was essential for any aspiring artist, whether Russian or American. Yehudi Menuhin made his debut in Berlin in 1929 when he was thirteen, although he had performed earlier in Paris and San Francisco. The photo files of the Berlin publishing house of Ullstein, now Springer Verlag, still contain pictures of the Menuhin children as performers as well as photographs of the young Jascha Heifetz in velvet knickers and ruffled shirt.

It is not surprising that classical musicians were middle-class. The obituary of the romantic pianist Shura Cherkassky, on December 29, 1995, in the *New York Times* gives an idea of the costs involved. He was born in Odessa in 1911 and gave concerts in that city when he was nine years old. By the time he left for New York at the age of eleven, he already had a professional manager as well as the advice of his mother. Sergei Rachmaninoff suggested that the boy should not give any concerts for two years and should study with Rosina Lhevinne, advice that was rejected. He had his debut in Baltimore when he was twelve. The profits of a child performer were large, but only middle-class or wealthy parents could afford the initial investment of training and preparing for concerts.

Child prodigies were all the rage. Horowitz gave his first performance at the age of eight, and he told how he had to make money to support his family after his father's business was ruined during the Russian Revolution. John Joachim provoked protests in the United States because "they were exploiting a child." It is interesting to note that none of these child performers seemed to be hurt by their early appearances and usually went on to long and illustrious musical careers. Many of them continued playing until they were well into their seventies or eighties.

While many of the performers were Jewish, only a few of the concert musicians had parents who were rabbis or cantors. The cantorial tradition of Solomon Sulzer of Vienna or Phinchas Minkowsky and David Novakovsky of the Broder synagogue in Odessa seldom intersected with that of performers on the concert stage. Shlomo Carlebach of New York did give concert performances, but they were of cantoral, not secular music.

Most Jewish concert musicians played stringed instruments or piano. Woodwinds, brass, or percussion instruments had far fewer Jewish practitioners. Perhaps this is due to the fact that the latter instruments were primarily used in military bands, a group that did not welcome Jews. On the other hand, composing music and conducting orchestras were areas open to Jews as well as non-Jews. Jewish composers came from many countries. Ernest Bloch was a Swiss; Aaron Copland and Leonard Bernstein were Americans. Paul Ducas, who wrote the *Sorcerer's Apprentice*, was a Frenchman, Sigmund Romberg of operetta fame was Hungarian, and Gustav Mahler was an Austrian. The Eastern European listing among conductors is long. The Damrosch clan of musicians and musicologists originated in Poznanz (Posen). Serge Koussevitzky, Andre Kostalanetz, and Ossip Gabrilovitch of the Detroit Symphony and Vladimir Golschman of the St. Louis Symphony all came from Russia. Among the Jewish conductors not from Russia one must certainly list Otto Klemperer from Berlin and Erich Leinsdorf from Vienna.

Citizenship and national origin had little to do with music, and performers moved readily from country to country, driven by economic opportunity or political oppression. Few of them denied their Jewish origin, but with very few exceptions, they played little role in the Jewish community. There was little Jewish nationalism in what they played. Jewish artists performed compositions by Jewish composers such as Mendelssohn, Meyerbeer, and Halevy but also played music by such well-known anti-Semites as Richard Wagner and Richard Strauss. Musical nationalism, most strongly urged by Adolf Hitler but also by other European nationalists—creating and performing "national music" that appealed to patriotic themes or heroic patriotic figures—had little attraction for Jewish musicians, although there have been some compositions based on traditional Jewish religious themes. However, Jewish performers did provide a network of composers, music directors, and virtuosos who favored their fellow countrymen. Today newly arrived Russian musicians have almost totally replaced the original Israelis in the orchestras of Israel.[10]

The history of Western Europe created opportunities for Jews to enter and prosper in the field of music. There had been a strong musical tradition at one time in Western Europe. The Germanic and Celtic chieftains maintained harpers at their courts; these players were not only musicians but also preservers of history, advisors, and interpreters of traditional law. In late medieval times, troubadours and minnesingers, love-song singers, wandered from court to court and castle to castle. Even a heroic king like Richard the Lion-Hearted of England was known to compose songs and was a close friend of his gleeman.[11]

Music also played a role in the peasant festivals of that time. Wandering fifers played recorders; lutists and drummers played for dances and harvest festivals and performed as entertainers in taverns. Military drummers and horn players accompanied the armies. At carnivals and similar festivals, amateur musicians joined in the music making. The Venetian painter Paolo Veronese painted himself playing the violincello and his fellow painter, Titian, playing contrabass in his *Wedding at Cana*, now in the Louvre in Paris. At about the same time, musicians were painted in peasant scenes by Pieter Breughel in the Lowlands.

However, around 1500 a strong religious reforming movement arose in Western Europe that frowned on all dancing and music except church music. In Florence, Savonarola, monk and de facto dictator, burnt violas, lutes, and harps together with paintings and perfumes in his "Bonfires of the Vanities." In Spain and the Netherlands, the Holy Office of the Inquisition looked with dour suspicion on dancing and nonchurch music as showing traces of paganism and Moorish influence.

In Protestant northern Europe, secular music fared no better than in the Catholic South. Luther composed powerful hymns but frowned upon both court musicians and peasant fifers. Perhaps some of his opposition to the peasant fifers comes from the fact that some of them had become leaders in the peasant revolts, which Luther opposed strongly indeed.[12] When Queen Mary of Scotland, around the same time in history, dared to make David Rizzio, a musician, her confidant, the Protestant Scottish nobles murdered him in the Queen's presence. Miles Standish of Massachusetts led his Puritan musketeers to attack the neighboring English settlement of Merrymount, where they had dared to dance around the maypole.

It is no surprise, therefore, that most Western European composers of this period turned out volumes of masses, oratorios, hymns, and other church music. Only in marginal Western Europe, in the Scottish Highlands, Ireland, and the Alps did the old musical tradition survive.[13]

Very little of this wave of austere reform touched the areas of Eastern Europe. From 1541 to nearly 1700, most of Hungary, the Balkans, the Ukraine, and southern Poland was under Turkish suzerainty. The Bukovina, now Romania, where many Jews lived, did not come under the Austrian government until 1783, and Bulgaria as well as Greece and Serbia did not join Western Europe as independent countries until even later. The Turks did not object to music, even non-Mohammedan music. As a result, bands of Gypsy and Jewish musicians flourished. They played at weddings, funerals, or any other festivities, and their music blended many sources of melody. These Jewish musicians were the *klezmer* bands, a term the dictionary simply defines as wandering musicians.[14] Jewish culture encouraged this music, and recently there has been a strong revival of klezmer music, played by non-Jewish as well as Jewish musicians.[15] The Hasidim included song and dance in their religious observances, and the Torah was often chanted in religious schools as part of the learning process.[16] Hazzans and cantors were part of the services in most synagogues. Music was also part of the course of instruction in secular Jewish schools, and even among the Orthodox, secular music was banned only on the Sabbath.

In such an atmosphere, there could be no objection to itinerant musicians. These might be a single fiddler or a band of twenty instrument players. They performed in public, on the streets of the Jewish quarter, and in the taverns, a fact that ensured that music was a familiar part of Eastern European living. As Shalem Aleichem pointed out, most boys in the ghetto at one time or another thought of owning a fiddle.[17]

By the middle of the seventeenth century, most courts and noblemen in Western Europe did maintain orchestras, but the status of the musician seldom rose above that of a very minor court official. Johann Sebastian Bach achieved the position of Royal Prussian bandmaster late in life and with great difficulty. Handel, despite his position as the British royal court composer, deposited the manuscript of his great oratorio, *The Messiah*, at the London Foundling Hospital. The problems of the adult Mozart, Schubert, and Beethoven in earning enough to keep body and soul together are well known. Their compositions are often dedicated to noblemen who either commissioned them or from whom the composer hoped to obtain patronage.

By the nineteenth century, young ladies in many Christian households were encouraged to acquire some skill on the pianoforte or harp and perhaps to sing well. However, the etiquette books of the period stressed that music should be neither too loud nor too long so that it wouldn't interfere with conversation.[18] Still later, the ideal function of a middle-class musician in a non-Jewish home was to accompany songs sung by a family group or a church choir. Male musicians, singers, and good dancers were considered to be not quite manly, and playing an instrument or singing in a glee club could be a bar to advancement in business or the military as late as the middle of the twentieth century.[19]

All of this left much room for the Jewish musicians. They seldom aspired to high social status, and "manliness" in the sense of fist fighting or shining in team athletics was mostly blocked to them in any case. Virtuoso musicians were acceptable in most parts of society as special cases, performers who required neither birth nor wealth nor even necessarily good manners. Genius was its own excuse, and if genius was well paid, so much the better. Promoters were quick to exploit the public desire for colorful performers and made sure that eccentricities, exotic backgrounds, and child prodigies were profitably exploited. Of course, there were many classical musicians who neither were nor desired to be virtuosos. Orchestras of twenty to one hundred players performed weekly in concert halls and opera houses. Unlike virtuosos, regular orchestra members had steady work without a retinue of agents and publicity managers and the endless, uncomfortable travel from city to city that was part of the life of soloists. In orchestras, too, there was a heavy representation of Jews from Russia and Hungary.

Another area of musical performance that must be mentioned is informal or private concerts. Trios and quartets met in private houses to play for the sheer joy of music. Some of these musicians were professionals and some were amateurs, like Albert Einstein, but the quality of music produced by these groups in the Jewish bourgeois homes in both Eastern and Western European cities was almost invariably of high quality. Sometimes an audience of musical connoisseurs was invited to a private home for an evening of music.[20]

In the period 1890–1940, there was hardly a cafe or a variety show that did not have musical performers or a small orchestra. This entertainment that took place in the daily world intersected hardly at all with the concert world. Strauss waltzes, parts of operettas and stage musicals, as well as occasional satiric pieces were standard fare. Gypsy music was also popular in the cafes. During the 1910–1920 period, dance halls were popular, places where respectable young men and women could meet each other and where social festivities by large families or fraternal groups could take place. Some of these dance halls were attached to hotels, but others were independent establishments. Again, many of the musicians in these dance halls came from Eastern European countries.[21]

Until very recently, the performing music world was an almost exclusively male domain. There were a few women singers, harpists, and harpsichordists, but practically no women playing other instruments in the orchestras. In an obituary of the pianist Heida

Hermanns, who died on the same date as Shura Cherkassy, her debut was noted as taking place in Town Hall, New York, when she was thirty-six years old. Female soloists, like the pianist Myra Hess and the Polish-born harpsichordist Wanda Landowski, became well known only in the post–World War II era. This is certainly not due to lack of female talent. The sister of Vladimir Horowitz and the sister of Yehudi Menuhin are noted as having as much talent as their brothers. Gradually, however, the women sink first to the status of accompanist, and finally disappear from the stage altogether. One field that was open to female musicians was the area of teaching. In some cases this meant placing the unformed fingers of small children on the piano keys, but in others women teachers stood behind virtuosos as teachers and advisors. This pattern now seems to be in a process of change. Women are being seen as performers on all instruments in orchestras and as soloists. Another change is an increasing number of Oriental performers replacing the Eastern European musicians.

NOTES

1. *New York Times*, Nov. 5, 1944, p. 15.

2. The Dreyfus case aroused international attention and tore France into two factions. The basic issue was one of anti-Semitic prejudice.

3. Ezra Mendelsohn, "On the Jewish Presence in Nineteenth-Century European Musical Life," in *Studies in Contemporary Judaism*, Vol. 9 ed. Ezra Mendelsohn (New York: Oxford University Press, 1994), p. 4.

4. Ibid.

5. Virgil Thompson, *A Virgil Thompson Reader* (Boston: 1981), p. 549.

6. Mendelsohn, p. 9.

7. Glenn Plaskin, *Horowitz* (New York: Morrow, 1983), p. 19.

8. Arthur Rubinstein, *My Young Years* (New York: Knopf, 1973), p. 7.

9. Quoted in Susanne Everett, *Lost Berlin* (New York: Bison Books, 1979), p. 110.

10. *New York Times*, Nov. 5, 1994, p. 15.

11. The tradition is that Blondel, Richard's gleeman, found the place where his king was imprisoned by singing Richard's favorite song outside various castles and waiting for Richard's response with a second verse.

12. Among the musicians who were leaders of the peasant revolts were the Fifer Hans of Nicholstadt, who was burned by the bishop of Würzburg, and the Fifer of Hart, who was a leader of the revolt of the Poor Conrad against the Duke of Würtemberg.

13. Clan McKinnon were the traditional pipers for the Clan MacDonald of Sleat, for instance. For music in alpine villages, see Philip V. Bohlman, "Musical Life in a Jewish Central European Village," in *Studies in Contemporary Judaism*, Vol. 9, ed. Ezra Mendelsohn (New York: Oxford University Press, 1994).

14. For an extensive study of the blending of musical traditions and melodies see A. Z. Idelsohn, *Jewish Music* (New York: Schocken Books, 1967).

15. The Klezmatics, a New York *klezmer* group, combines historical research with modern improvization. They include both Jewish and non-Jewish musicians. Similar groups are popular in Berlin and even in Poland.

16. Lionel Wolberger, "Music in Holy Argument," in *Studies in Contemporary Judaism*, Vol. 9, ed. Ezra Mendelsohn (New York: Oxford University Press, 1994).

17. Shalom Aleichem, *The Fiddle*, 1946, p. 301.

18. Anonymous, *Hints on Etiquette* (1836; reprint, New York: E. P. Dutton, 1951), p. 35.

19. "That's Skid Gabriel playing the piano. Again I thought about Muriel's theory about music and the army. The officer was only a major." John P. Marquand, *Melville Goodwin USA* (Boston: Little, Brown, 1951), p. 517.

20. The quality of such informal music groups can be demonstrated even as late as during the Holocaust, when an informal

group of musicians produced the opera *The Emperor of Atlantis* in the Terezin concentration camp. The opera was performed after the war in Amsterdam and New York. Joza Karas, *Music in Terezin* (Stuyvesant, N.Y.: Pendragon Press, 1985).

21. My wife's grandfather, of Hungarian Jewish background, owned three of these dance halls at one time; see illustration. He also managed a band of Eastern European musicians in which he played the violin.

7

From Badkhen to Hollywood

The most elaborate and joyous festival in stetl life was a wedding. Every bride was as beautifully dressed as possible and pointed out to the children of the village as someone to envy. The groom was invited to sleep in the richest man's house so he would have at least one night about which he could dream in the future. There was always enough food at a wedding, not only enough to eat at the time but also enough for everyone to take something home.

A wedding was a staged village fantasy in which all inhabitants participated, knowing that the everyday world was not like this.[1] An indispensable figure in a large wedding in Eastern Europe was the jester, the *badkhen*, who usually also served as the master of ceremonies. He was present with the musicians as the guests assembled. He was the one who treated the bride to a discourse on her duties as a wife. Throughout the festivities, the badkhen was at hand to move the company to laughter and to tears. Weeping was expected and encouraged, weeping by the bride, weeping by the mothers of both the bride and the groom, even weeping by the fathers, who bemoan what they are losing. There was also laughter, laughter about the in-laws and their families, discussions of the wedding gifts, and sly jokes about the wedding guests, village affairs, and even the government, all of the humor carefully manipulated by the badkhen so as not to give real offense. At his highest, his performance combined the skill of an actor, poet, singer, and commentator. A really great badkhen was widely known and constantly in demand.[2]

A badkhen was a professional who sold entertainment. His social status in the community was not high; he didn't rate with the rich or with the learned, but he associated with those who did have high status in the community. Like the *shadkhen*, the marriage broker, he was a man whom it was wise not to offend.

The fantasies of the Eastern Jewish wedding feast and the skills of the badkhen in creating the changing mood of the festivities became, when they moved westward, the fantasies and mood manipulation of the entertainment industry, especially of the movies. The creators of the movie industry were almost all Jews from Poland, Russia, and Hungary, from small villages and poor social and economic background.[3] All of them came from a 500-mile circle centered on Warsaw. Their fathers were mostly luftmenschen. Benjamin Warner, whose sons Harry, Sam, Albert, and Jack Warner built Warner Brothers, was a cobbler from Poland who settled in Youngstown, Ohio. Louis B. Mayer, later head of MGM, had been exploited by his father, a scrap-metal dealer in Boston who had emigrated from Russia. Marcus Loew was a drummer, a travelling salesman of textiles who acquired his first movie house in Covington, Kentucky. Dick Schenk, who took over MGM from Loew, owned a pharmacy with his brother in New York City. He came to the movies by way of the ownership of an amusement park in northern Manhattan. He later was a partner of Loew in the Palisades Amusement Park, which survived World War II. Adolph Zukor, an orphan from a village in Hungary, was a furrier, and Sam Goldwyn, born Smuel Gelbfisz, was an illegal immigrant from

Warsaw who first made and then sold ladies' gloves in Gloversville, New York.

None of these individuals were young men when they started in the movie industry. They had been merchants and mostly small-town people with strong roots in Eastern European culture. When they did enter the new field of the movies, they built their business in the traditional ghetto manner, trusting to their instincts and nerve. They seldom relied on lawyers, bankers, or other advisors. When they needed business associates or partners, they first went to the people they knew, relatives or former business associates. Their feuds were as bitter as their friendships were intense. They distrusted and fought the non-Jewish establishment, whether that establishment was represented by the banks or the Edison Trust, which tried to control their moviemaking. Edison Trust claimed to be able to control moviemaking by virtue of its patents on the movie camera and film, but Jewish filmmakers evaded the enforcement detectives, buying their photographic film from overseas or disguising the cameras they were using. Win or lose, the moviemakers in the early days were individualists using their ghetto skills on a larger scale.

Like the character of Tevye in *Fiddler on the Roof*,[4] the moviemaker fantasized about his life "if [he] were a rich man." When filmmakers did become very rich, they built the fantasy world we know as Hollywood. The way the fantasies of these these new, rich producers, moguls, and actors were acted out, as well as the hard-nosed, cut-throat business practices of the industry, gave Hollywood a bad name for immorality of all kinds in the America of 1919–1923. This was the period when America was struggling to "return to normalcy," when prohibition was introduced and the first restrictions on immigration were put in place. Yet Hollywood and the movie industry had become so important in America that the U.S. House of Representatives and the Senate passed a joint resolution asking the moviemakers to make films to "upbuild and strengthen the spirit of Americanism" in 1919. To protect themselves and their products from local censorship initiatives and anti-Semitic attacks, the movie moguls brought in a non-Jew, William H. Hays, to set up a code of what could and could not be shown on the silver screen. Mr. Hays had been chairman of the national committee of the Republican party and postmaster general in the Harding administration. It was hoped that his moral decorum would make the movies acceptable to the Main Streets of Christian America.

In the movies profanity, hot kisses and bare bosoms were out, but Hollywood itself remained one of the most tolerant communities in the United States. The movie company bosses, outsiders themselves, cared nothing about the religion, ethnic background, drink and drug dependencies, or extramarital affairs of their co-moguls and employees as long as they did their job well and kept their sins private. As in the ghettos from which they had sprung, business came first. However, the activities of actors, actresses, and directors were the material for gossip columnists, and the arrests for drunkenness and the various love partnerships appeared in all the newspapers of the country. This meant that private lives did affect business, and soon a morals clause was inserted into every acting contract. Because of the gossip columnists and the personal relationships in what was actually a fairly small community, it was important to be seen and talked about. Who you knew and what was gossiped about you were often factors in obtaining work or an important role in a film. The gossip factor and the personal relationships were similar to those that governed the old stetl.

On October 7, 1927, Al Jolson, a cantor's son born Asa Yaelson, spoke words from a movie screen.[5] From then on the accents of the actors and actresses mattered. Moviemakers started the hunt for the clipped voices of Englishmen, for Hungarians who could speak like counts, for gravel-voiced cowboys and villains. However, not everybody took part in this trend of ethnic correctness. Eddie Cantor remained what he had always been, a Jewish comedian, as did Danny Kaye and Jerry Lewis. Charlie Chaplin remained silent as always. However, most actors became the kind of characters that they portrayed on the screen, and Jewish dominance in the acting field diminished. There were even some anti-Semites employed in Hollywood; Walt Disney and Adolphe Menjou had that reputation. This was to have serious consequences at a later date.

Of course, Hollywood was not the only part of the entertainment world where Jews played a large role. Their dominance in the classical music field was described in the last chapter. Jews like Solomon Hurok, born near Gomel in Poland, became a potent force in booking stage entertainment. His first job was a manager and booking agent for a Socialist party center in Brownsville, Brooklyn. Among his performers was the violinist Ephraim Zimbalist, whom Hurok convinced to donate part of his fee to the Socialist party.[6] From Brooklyn Hurok moved to the New York Hippodrome at Forty-third Street and Sixth Avenue. He attracted crowds to see and hear his performers, including ballet dancers and opera stars, by advertising in Yiddish and other ethnic papers, with specific instructions on how to get from the ethnic enclaves to downtown by subway or trolley. For Hurok, too, ethnic origin or moral rectitude was of no importance. Only artistic performance counted. Other Jewish promoters were also active in arranging stage performances, one of the best known being Ziegfeld, who produced the Ziegfeld Follies. Also important were movie house owners like Belasco, Balaban, and Katz, as well as the flamboyant "Roxy" (Samuel Rothapfel). The latter included a symphony orchestra and a ballet with a Russian ballet master to supplement the movie performances in the Roxy movie house.[7]

The worlds of entertainment in New York and in Hollywood increasingly merged. The best stage plays and drama writers came to Hollywood. Movie palaces with their gilding and red velvet formed the image of what real palaces are like for most Americans.[8] Actors, singers, and musicians appeared on the stages of these "palaces." The big bands, Benny Goodman, Harry James, Gene Krupa, and many others attracted large crowds to the Paramount in New York. Judy Garland made a personal appearance at the same time as her *Wizard of Oz* was shown on the screen. The most elaborate and probably the last of these giant movie theaters was

Radio City Music Hall, which opened in New York in 1932. It had a symphony orchestra to play light music, a corps de ballet, and the famous chorus line of the Rockettes. Radio City Music Hall is still open, and the stage shows still attract crowds, but it no longer shows films.

The Wall Street crash of 1929 affected the movie industry just as it affected the rest of the country. To salvage their companies, many movie studios turned increasingly to bankers, bookkeepers, and business managers. Dr. Giannini of the Bank of Italy (later Bank of America) was already deeply involved in financing movie-making and even served temporarily as United Artists' president. Other non-Jews came into the field as investors, directors, and producers, but the popular conception of the Hollywood film industry remained predominantly Jewish.

To go to the movies on Saturday night was the normal activity for American teenagers—but not only teenagers. By 1916 the average weekly attendance at the movies was 10 million viewers. By 1937 the average weekly figure was to reach an astounding 80 million.[9] The movies defined much of America both in this country and overseas. If that image was a good part fantasy, it was accepted, and like the fantasy of an Eastern European Jewish wedding, it was an image that everybody liked to believe, most of the time. After the harsh experiences of World War II, the Hollywood fantasy began to fade and realism made its presence felt in the movies shown to America.

Creating the image of America was a long way to come for the group of Eastern European immigrants who conceived and distributed the films. They had become a kind of royalty, received as important figures by the heads of European states, pampered by hoteliers and headwaiters everywhere. Yet the moguls ran their studios with an iron hand, making and unmaking stars and directors. Movie moguls associated with the top artists and intellectuals of the day, often hiring them to work on their films. If a certain crudeness of accent remained among some of the movie producers, and some of the intellectuals sneered at their product as *kitsch*, artistic and financial acumen brought these immigrants a long way from the ghettos and villages of their birth.

But the ghettos that agents like Sol Hurok of New York and moviemaker Sam Goldwyn of California had left behind followed them to America. The rise of Hitler in Germany brought a flood of European artists to Hollywood. Erich Maria Remarque, Vicki Baum, Franz Werfel, Berthold Brecht, and Arnold Schoenberg were among the 59 German screenwriters, 33 directors and 19 composers working in the movie industry.[10] Perhaps even more disturbing to many of the entertainment kings were the desperate letters they were getting from relatives, close or distant, they had left behind in Europe. Sam Goldwyn tried to get his sister and her husband out of Poland in 1939, but they stayed too long and died in the extermination camp at Treblinka.[11] The tale was similar for many others. Carl Laemmle helped over 250 German Jews come to the United States until he was informed that his affidavits would no longer be accepted by the U.S. immigration authorities. Adolph Zukor's brother, who had become a rabbi in Berlin, fled to Palestine.[12] In 1936 a number of Hollywood figures created the Anti-Nazi League. With so many Jews and anti-Nazi refugees, there were few illusions about what Hitler was and meant to do. Charlie Chaplin's film *The Great Dictator* was only one of the many efforts to alert America about the Nazi menace.

Anti-Semitism was rising in America at the same time as the anti-Nazi movement. Many of the members of the anti-Semitic group and their allies, the isolationist conservatives, attacked the entertainment industry for its anti-Hitler attitude. In 1940 Senator Nye of North Dakota proclaimed that the movies were agitating for war. "In each movie company there are a number of production directors, many of them who have come from Russia, Hungary, Germany and the Balkan countries—people who are naturally subject to racial emotions."[13] Joseph P. Kennedy, ex-ambassador to Britain, warned the movie executives in a private meeting: "The war is being seen as a Jewish war. . . . You're going to have to get those Jewish names off the screen."[14] Pearl Harbor intervened before Hollywood could decide whether to yield to such pressures. While America was at war, Hollywood was not only free to make antifascist pictures but officially encouraged to do so. But the hatred and anti-Semitism went underground only temporarily.

Right after the end of the war, in 1946, Congressman Rankin reopened the attack on Hollywood. "They want to spread their un-American propaganda as well as their loathsome, lying, immoral anti-Christian filth before the eyes of children."[15]

The beginning of the cold war and the anti-Communist hysteria of the time gave the right wingers a convenient target. It was not necessary to be a member of the Communist party or even one of the many Communist front organizations; the accusation of "following the Communist line" was sufficient to damn anyone. In the debate over the citation for contempt of Congress by the "Hollywood Ten," a group of uncooperative witnesses accused of being sympathetic to Communism by the House Un-American Activities Committee, Congressman Rankin read off a series of names.

"One of the names is June Havoc. We found out her real name is June Havick. Another is Danny Kaye. We found out his real name is David Daniel Kamisky. Another is Eddie Cantor, whose real name is Edward Israel Iskowitz. There is one who calls himself Edward Robinson. His real name is Emmanuel Goldberg."[16]

To people like Representative Rankin, being Jewish was the same as being Communist. Much of Hollywood yielded to the new pogrom, including some of the Jewish executives. Led by Jack Warner, they cooperated fully and voluntarily in the purge of suspected Communists. Not only were the ten uncooperative witnesses fired under the morality clause in their contract, but many other writers, actors, and directors lost their jobs and were blacklisted, thus barred from finding any other employment in Hollywood. Often the only evidence against them was an accusation of political incorrectness by some self-appointed committee or an American Legion post. Of course, some of the accused were indeed leftists or, like Hanns Eisler the composer, involved in actual Communist espionage. The political purge was, of course, not confined to Hollywood but was carried on equally in newspapers, on college campuses, and in business firms.[17]

The kings of entertainment found that they were still not accepted as members of the American majority. They were fiddlers and badkhens, entertainers who were highly paid and desirable for what they were skilled in doing, but no matter what their fame, they were not part of the elite governing group. If they offended the real leaders of the community, they lost their jobs, just as in Eastern Europe. It was a bitter lesson that has not been forgotten by most of the older Jews today, leaving many of them careful not to stray too far from the opinions of the majority of the population, while turning others into bitter rebels. This is similar to the experience of the Jews of Eastern Europe around the turn of the last century.

Not all the badkhens had gone to Hollywood nor graduated into the top money earners in America. Many still functioned as masters of ceremonies and entertainers at weddings, small night clubs, and in Jewish vacation resorts. Others performed on the stage, like Jackie Mason and Danny Kaye.[18] Here the old routines, the old Jewish jokes and sly Jewish commentaries on Eastern Europe still reigned. In the Jewish wedding "palaces" that dot the suburbs of New York City and elsewhere the badkhen is still needed and desired and plays his traditional role.

NOTES

1. The wedding feast has been transplanted to America and has become even more elaborate and expensive. It is not unusual for a father of the bride to spend a year's income on his daughter's wedding. Many girls prefer the fancy wedding to receiving the same amount of money for their living expenses or a wedding trip.

2. Mark Zborowski and Elizabeth Herzog, *Life Is With People* (New York: International University Press, 1952), p. 278.

3. Carl Laemmle, founder of Universal Pictures, came from the village of Laupheim in southwestern Germany, population

about 3,000, and was the only German Jew among the early Hollywood pioneers.

4. Sheldon Harnick, "If I Were a Rich Man," in *Fiddler on the Roof*, by Joseph Stein based on stories by Shalom Aleichem, New York, RCA recording LOC 1093.

5. This film, *The Jazz Singer*, dealt with the conflict between the traditional Jewish role as cantor and the wish for a Broadway career for the cantor's son.

6. Sol Hurok (with Ruth Goode), *Impresario, a Memoir* (New York: Random House, 1946), p. 24.

7. Neal Gabler, *An Empire of Their Own* (NewYork: Doubleday, 1989), p. 100.

8. The first movie "palace" was the Strand on Forty-second Street in New York, which opened in 1915.

9. Figures from Gene Brown, *Movie Time* (New York: Macmillan, 1995).

10. James K. Lyon, *Berthold Brecht in America* (London: Methuen, 1982), p. 46.

11. A. Scott Berg, *Goldwyn* (New York: Knopf, 1989), p. 345.

12. Gabler, p. 344.

13. Ibid., p. 345.

14. Berg, p. 346; also recorded in Gabler, p. 344.

15. Quoted in Gabler, p. 358.

16. Ibid., p. 379.

17. There were a large number of Un-American Activities Committees on private, state, and federal levels. Some of the better-known chairmen of the national committees were J. Parnell Thomas and Martin Dies. In New York State the committee was usually known as the Rapp-Coudert committee after the chairmen of the Assembly and state Senate committees. Public anti-Semitism in Congress was openly expressed not only by Congressman Rankin but also by Senator Bilbo, also from Mississippi.

18. Danny Kaye played the character Noah in *Two by Two* and the Jew Jacobowsky in *Me and the Colonel*.

8

Images of the Ghetto

"Yiddish in my time was an empty vessel. . . . The women and the commonest people read the stuff. Other people were ashamed to read Yiddish, not wanting to show their backwardness. The Hebrew writers despised Yiddish and mocked it. . . . This was my dilemma for if I wrote in this 'unworthy' language my honor would be besmirched. . . . I would have pity for Yiddish, that rejected daughter, for it was time to do something for our people. I fell in love with Yiddish and wedded her forever."[1] Thus wrote Sholem Jacob Abromovich, better known as Mendele the Bookseller (*Mendele Mokher Sforim*). The sentiment is in line with the sentiments of the Russian *Narodny*, those who, like Count Tolstoy, wanted to go back to the people.[2] Mendele published his first Yiddish story in 1864. More stories followed, and Mendele is often considered the grandfather of the Yiddish storytellers.

The other founders of the classical Yiddish story genre are I. L. Peretz (1852–1915), who published his first Yiddish story in 1890, and Sholem Rabinowitz (1859–1916), better known as Sholem

Aleichem. His most famous character, Tevye the Milkman, made his appearance in literature around 1890 as well.

These three authors and the others who joined their movement shared a belief in the goodness of the poor Jews of the ghetto. They took the part of the poor and oppressed against the rich and often the part of the Hasidim against the established rabbis. Yet these writers were not part of the lower classes themselves but of a solid bourgeois background. Peretz, for instance, was a trained lawyer. Their audience was also mostly bourgeois: teachers, lawyers, merchants, and accountants, as well as some of the new Jewish proletariat of the cities of Poland, the Ukraine, and Galicia. The poor ghetto dweller had no money for books and knew the ghetto life all too well from firsthand experience to want to read about it. The Yiddish readers who had divorced themselves from the stetl needed these stories. These stories gave them a connection with the culture of small-town and village Jews, romanticized a bit perhaps, but with its flavor and characters intact. They had trouble acculturating to the cities and even more trouble acculturating to the dominant Christian society of the city, finding that the stetl was more human than the cities in which they lived and worked.

From Eastern Europe these stories flowed westward to Vienna, from Budapest to Geneva, the city of political exiles, and especially to Berlin. They gained enormously in popularity, often in translation from Yiddish to German or English. The sentiments and the love of the common people expressed by these writers went well with the sentiments of the rising Zionist movement, especially with the program of the Democratic Faction of Zionists, who called for a Jewish cultural revival as well as a religious revival. Klezmer music, Jewish folklore, and Yiddish language created a romantic package that found ready acceptance. The sentiment of these stories also appealed to Socialists and members of the anti-Zionist Bund, since part of the Bund program sponsored Yiddish and the poor against the Hebrew speakers, the orthodox rabbis, and the rich.

Berlin became the center of Jewish publishing in the early twentieth century, because of both a lack of censorship and low costs.

Berlin saw the founding of the Jewish Publishing House, which was created by Chaim Weizmann, Martin Buber, the Galician-born artist Ephraim Moses Lillian, and the translator Berthold Feiwel. Other publishing houses turning out Hebrew and Yiddish books soon followed. The Jewish Publishing House issued inexpensive editions of Herzl's writings, Buber's Hasidic tales, and Morris Rosenfeld's *Songs of the Ghetto*, previously published in New York. Berthold Feiwel, who also functioned as friend and political ally of Weizmann, carefully explained that Rosenfeld had used the Yiddish based on German dialects, not the Yiddish of Poland or New York's East Side.[3] This was to make the book more acceptable to German-Jewish audiences, who resisted any identification with the poor and the orthodox Eastern Jews who inhabited the Scheunenviertel together with prostitutes and fences for stolen goods. The Scheunenviertel retained its influence over Jewish writers who wrote in German as well. Franz Kafka taught there in a settlement house. The actor Alexander Granach perfected his Shylock by returning to the bakery in the Scheunenviertel where he had worked before. Edwin Piscator, the famous German director, produced his *Kaufmann von Berlin* based on characters drawn from the Scheunenviertel. This play, directed by Maholy-Nagy with music by Hanns Eisler, was a succès de scandale. It was condemned by the Jews as anti-Semitic, by the German nationalists as slanderous of German officers, and by the Communists as being bourgeois.[4]

New York had its Yiddish printing houses and publishers as well. Sholem Aleichem was an honored author when he arrived in New York in 1906, but there was little market for his writings or those of other Yiddish authors, even in translation. The "uptown" Jews, mostly German Jews, wanted desperately to leave behind the ghettos from which they had come. They did not want to identify themselves with the Lower East Side Jews, just as the Jews living in Berlin's West Side wanted as little as possible to do with the Scheunenviertel. The Jews of Frankfurt, Germany, had originated in the small villages of the Rhineland, and they as well as their descendants considered themselves infinitely superior to the Jews from the East. The Jews of Vienna and Budapest often tried to be super-Austrians, even when their parents had come to Vienna or Budapest from the Hungarian countryside, the Bukovina, or Galicia. Even under the Nazis, there was still hostility between the Latvian Jews and the German Jews in the Riga ghetto.[5] This artificial separation of the Jewish communities was not to close until after World War II and the Holocaust.[6]

Yiddish theater, also romanticizing the poor and the Hasidim of the ghettos, rose at the same time as Yiddish literature. The Yiddish plays were derived from the *purimspiel*,[7] the performances that were traditionally part of the *Purim* holiday. In 1866 the Brody Singers, named after the city of their origin, were already performing in nightclubs and cabarets. By 1876, there were Yiddish plays, written by Abraham Goldfaden, being performed for the Russian officers who were in Romania fighting the war against Turkey. These plays dealt with the problems of the ghetto poor and were often performed by actors in Hasidic costume. The same Hasidic costume was seized upon by cartoonists and publishers of anti-Semitic postcards in Hungary.

From Romania, Yiddish plays and acting groups spread all over Russia and Poland. In 1882, when some of the Yiddish playwrights in Russian territories had moved toward more serious themes than in ghetto comedies, the tsarist police banned all Jewish theater groups and performances. Many of the Yiddish playwrights moved to New York's Bowery.[8] Jewish plays, whether in Yiddish or Hebrew, would not revive in Poland or Russia until after the end of World War I and the overthrow of the tsar.

The invention of the movies created a Yiddish-speaking movie industry in Warsaw and New York that continued to produce films until 1940. As Yiddish speakers died out, so did the Yiddish movie industry. Some of these films have now been reproduced for television viewing.

The interest in the culture of the ghettos was supported by scientific ethnographic research among the Jewish communities. Solomon Seinwill Rappaport, better known as Sh An-Ski, author of the famous play *The Dybbuk*, collected material for his three-volume *The Destruction of the Jews of Poland, Galicia and the Bukovina* during World War I. Simon Dubnow collected ethnographic material and artifacts in Soviet times and wrote his *History of the Jews* from an ethnological and sociological rather than from a religious viewpoint. Part of his collection survived both Stalin and World War II and was recently shown in a museum in New York.

During the 1920–1930 period, the Jews of the ghetto were treated almost like a primitive tribe. Photographers like Ramon Vishniac, whose main field was scientific microscope photography, travelled through Poland and Romania in 1938, recording the people, the synagogues, and the yeshivas before all this was swept away by the invading Nazis.[9] He was not the only photographer active in recording ghetto life at the time.[10] YIVO, the Jewish Research Institute, was founded in Vilna, Lithuania, in 1925 and later moved to New York City.[11] Almost all the pictures we have of ghetto life come from this late period and give us a somewhat static image of life in the Jewish communities of Eastern Europe.

Also in the twentieth century, Marc Chagall created his visionary ghetto scenes, a world where rabbis, fiddlers, and stetl characters float in colorful landscapes. In this form the images were acceptable to collectors of art in the West. Chagall also created the setting for the Jewish theater in Moscow in 1922, a space that became known as Chagall's box. However, the researches of Dubnow, the paintings of Chagall, and much else of historical interest was hidden in attics and warehouses when the Communists began to condemn all Jewish culture as "bourgeois Jewish nationalism." Some of this material, including Chagall's theater canvases, has reappeared after the fall of the Soviet Union.

Many other Jewish artists from Russia also came westward in the 1920s, but most of them adopted a humanistic style rather than portraying the ghettos. In Paris one must mention Soutine, Jacques Lipschitz, and Chaim Gross. In New York there were the Soyer brothers and William Zorach, among many others. It is the variety of the work produced by these artists that has spawned the endless debates about the definition of Jewish art.

The Nazi era and the belated knowledge of the destruction not only of 6 million individual Jewish lives but also of all Jewish culture in Europe created a frantic hunt for roots on the part of those Jews who had survived the war in the safe havens of America and elsewhere.[12] The Yiddish stories of Shalom Aleichem, Sholem Asch, I. B. Singer, and others were translated into English and brought out by mass-market publishers. Tevye the Milkman moved to the Broadway stage as *Fiddler on the Roof*, and went from there to Hollywood. Artifacts of Jewish life, life histories, and photographs were carefully gathered and enshrined in museums and research libraries. This is true not only in the United States and Israel, but also in Hungary, Germany, the Czech Republic, and Poland. Even in many places where there are no more Jews, universities give courses in Jewish culture as well as the Hebrew and Yiddish languages.

The gas crematoria of Auschwitz, Treblinka and Maidanek destroyed much of the Jewish past and almost all of the past of the Eastern European ghetto. The cohesion of the family, the stories handed down, the memories of the towns of origin are gone, even though there are individual survivors. While Israel gives many Jews hope of a future, the past that was blotted out is missed by all.

The ghetto has disappeared in Europe, but many of its features are being re-created by the neo-Orthodox and Hasidim in Jerusalem and New York. One sees once more the fur hats, black coats, and side curls of the men and the women's *scheitl* of the old ghettos. Prosperity has banished the starvation and misery of the stetl, but the battle between the followers of the enlightenment, the followers of the way of the Hasidim, and the way of the Orthodox has risen again. The old debates about who is a "proper Jew" can be heard again in Jewish communities in Germany and the United States. The mass-market bookstores in New York stock the Talmud and its commentaries. The images of the ghetto and its heritage that date from before the Holocaust have become the fought-over inheritance of the Jews of today. As Israel becomes more a country in the Middle East and less an idealistic dream, the need for this heritage will increase. Today many adults go through the ceremonies of Bar Mitzvah, and Bat Mitzvah for women has become common. Jewish weddings celebrated in the United States today become increasingly similar to the weddings of the stetl, complete with bakhton, *koschre tanz*, and kosher food even among the non-Orthodox.

The heritage of the East has bridged the gap between the Jews of East and West, a gap that was always more a wish than a reality.

NOTES

1. Quoted in Gitelman, p. 116.

2. The *Narodny* movement, The Cause of the People, was founded by the Russian writer Lavrov while in exile in Geneva. He recommended that his followers help the peasants by dressing like them and working at similar jobs as the peasants. The Art and Crafts movement in the West also extolled the goodness and habits of the peasants.

3. Morris Rosenfeld, *Lieder des Ghettos*, trans. Berthold Feiwel (Berlin: Herrman Seeman, 1902).

4. Geisel, p. 66.

5. *Aufbau*, January 1996.

6. The organizations of survivors of the Holocaust and the various Holocaust museums, including the Yad Vashem in Jerusalem, make no distinction between the Eastern Jews and the German Jews who died in the extermination camps.

7. Chrone Shmeruk, "The Purimspil," in *Purim: The Face and the Mask* (New York: Yeshiva University Museum, 1979), p. 44.

8. Sanders, p. 307.

9. The author's father also photographed the Riga and Lublin ghettos while on a selling trip of advertising novelties in 1930.

10. Josh Waletzky (director), *Image Before My Eyes* Video, 1991, YIVO Institute for Jewish Research, distr. by Ergo Media, Teaneck, N.J.

11. The Vilna files of YIVO have been rediscovered and are being microfilmed by YIVO archivists and made available in New York.

12. The initial attempts of the Jews of Israel were to find their roots in the ancient Israel of biblical and Roman days. Now there is an increasing effort on the part of some Israelis to base themselves in the European traditions as well.

Glossary

Alliance Israelite Universelle: Jewish international organization founded in Paris in 1860 under Baron Rothschild to coordinate action on Jewish problems. Played a role in dealing with the problems of Russian refugees of the pogroms of 1880 and in early Zionist activity.

Ashkenazi: German Jews as well as their rites and customs, in contrast with the *Sephardim* originating in Spain and the Orient.

Badkhen: The jester and master of ceremonies at a Jewish wedding in Eastern Europe.

Bet Din: Jewish rabbinical court of justice.

Birobidjian: Jewish Autonomous Region in southern Siberia on the Chinese border. It was established by the Soviets in 1924 as an answer to Zionism. Birobidjian is still in existence.

Brühl: Street in Leipzig, Germany, that was the center of the international fur trade.

Bukovina: Austrian province from 1775 to 1918, now divided between Romania and the Ukraine. It was the home of many Jews.

Bund—Allgemeiner Yiddisher Arbeiterbund: Jewish workers' league formed in Poland and Russia in 1897. After the Russian Revolution, it split into Socialist and Communist wings.

Byzantium: Today Istanbul, Turkey. Formerly known as Constantinople. It was founded by Constantine the Great in 330 C.E. and stormed by the Ottoman Turks in 1453. It was the great trading center between Asia and Europe for 1,000 years.

Cantonists: Young Jewish draftees in the Russian army in the nineteenth century. They were placed in cantonements, or barracks, for indoctrination and training.

Cossacks: Bands of adventurers serving as light cavalry in the Russian army in return for local autonomy; formerly they considered themselves independent of any government. They are noted for their loyalty to the Russian Orthodox religion and, as soldiers, for cruelty and looting.

Extrakommando: Nazi special military unit charged with the extermination or shooting of Jews. Usually composed of second-line German troops, with Estonian, Latvian, Lithuanian, or Ukrainian auxiliary units, all commanded by SS officers.

Galicia: Province of Austria 1775–1918, now part of Poland. It is located north of the Carpathian Mountains on the Polish plain. It was the home of many Jews.

Ghetto: Restricted area of residence, especially for Jews. The name is derived from the Venetian living and trading area reserved for Jews.

Gulag: A forced labor camp in the Soviet Union, usually located in an isolated and unhealthy area.

Habsburg territories: The Habsburg dynasty ruled over Austria, Hungary, Bohemia (today Czech and Slovak republics), parts of Poland, parts of Western Germany, Belgium, northern Italy, and Spain. The last Habsburg emperor abdicated in 1918.

Hansa: League of merchant cities in medieval Europe extending from Antwerp to Novgorod. Maintained extraterritorial rights in cities like London.

Harredim: "They who tremble." Modern term for very orthodox Jews.

Hasidim: "The Pietists." Mystical Jewish religious movement originating in Poland in the eighteenth century. Now divided into various groups, each following their own dynasty of religious leaders. The different groups of Hasidim are known by the name of the town of origin of their leaders.

Haskala: "The Enlightenment." Jewish movement originating in Germany in the eighteenth century advocating a knowledge of modern languages and science combined with Jewish religion.

Holocaust: The policy and practice of the Nazi government of destroying all Jews and Jewish culture in Europe, 1933–1945.

Holy Office of the Inquisition: Catholic agency founded in Spain to stamp out heresy and all traces of Judaism and Islam. It was known for the use of torture to induce confessions.

Industrial Revolution: The replacement of hand labor by machines in factories. The crucial developments of the Industrial Revolution included the invention of weaving machinery, steam engines, and railroads.

Jagellon dynasty: Kings of Poland, 1389–1696. After the death of the last member of this dynasty, the crown of Poland became elective.

Joachimsthaler: Large silver coin first minted by Count Schlick in Bohemia in 1520. It set the standard for most European silver coinage for centuries under the name of *thaler*, dollar or crown.

Kahilla: Jewish community having considerable powers of self-administration.

Kitsch: Objects of art in bad taste, being overdone or cheapened in some way.

Klezmer: Jewish folk music.

Kosher: Ritually clean according to Jewish religious law.

Kristallnacht: "Night of Broken Glass." November 9–10, 1938, when the Nazis destroyed all Jewish businesses and houses of worship.

Landsmannschaft: Organization of people coming from one region for purposes of mutual aid. A Landsmannschaft may or may not have its own synagogue.

Lower East Side: Area of New York City centered on Hester Street where most Eastern European Jews first settled. The Lower East Side also contained Irish, German, and Italian areas.

Luftmenschen: Jews who "live on air," that is, unemployed or marginally employed Jews.

Lumpenproletariat: "Ragged proletariat." The lowest level of the working class. The term was coined by Karl Marx.

Mammoth: Extinct member of the elephant family that lived in Siberia, Europe, and America during the last Ice Age. The tusks are still found, and are used for ivory.

Messe: Fair or market. Sometimes with attached name of product shown or town name. Otherwise, the fair at Leipzig is meant.

Mishnagadim: "The Opponents." Orthodox Jewish antagonists of the Hasidic movement.

Mizrachi: Movement of religious Zionism in opposition to the cultural Zionism advocated by the Democratic Faction headed by Chaim Weizmann.

New Economic Policy: Lenin's economic reforms, which allowed some capitalism, launched in 1924 and abolished by Stalin in

1927. This policy created a great deal of corruption in Russia and added the word *nep*, to cheat, to the Yiddish language.

Palestine: Geographic term for the Holy Land. Its borders depend on the speaker. In 1918, when the area was placed under British mandate, it included all of Israel and Jordan. Today the term is used for the Arab-controlled part of Israel.

Parnassim: The rich Jewish upper classes. The term is derived from the Greek Mt. Parnassus, reputed home of Apollo and the Muses.

Passover or Pesach: Jewish religious holiday celebrating the release of the Jews from Egyptian bondage.

Pogrom: Anti-Jewish riot or organized prosecution.

Proletariat: The working class, particularly industrial workers.

Purimspil: Plays or parodies performed at *purim*, the festival of Esther. The purimspil have been traced back to the sixteenth century.

Rabbi or *rebbe:* Originally meant a learned man, but is now used for ordained Jewish ministers.

Sabbath: The seventh day of the week, ordained for rest. The Jewish Sabbath runs from Friday sundown to Saturday sundown.

Scheitl: Wig worn by orthodox Jewish married women.

Scheunenviertel: Hay barn district. The slum district in central Berlin inhabited mainly by Eastern Jews from 1880 to 1938.

Sephardic: Jewish groups and ritual originating in Spain. After the expulsion of the Jews from Spain in 1492, many Sephardic Jews settled in the Turkish empire or in Amsterdam.

Shadkhen: Marriage broker.

Shadlan: Official or unofficial intermediary between the Jewish community and government officials.

Silesia: Prussian province 1757–1918, centered on the Oder River. It is noted for its coal and textile industries. Now part of Poland.

Spartakists: German communist group named after the leader of the slave revolt in Roman times. The Spartakists were led by Karl Liebknecht and Rosa Luxemburg. The Spartakist revolt in 1918 was put down by a coalition of militarists and the Social Democratic government.

Stetl: Small town or village in Eastern Europe inhabited by Jews.

Sweat shop: Small industrial plant or home workshop noted for its low wages and poor working conditions.

Talmud: Compilation of Jewish oral traditions collected after the destruction of the Temple in Jerusalem by the Romans in 73 C.E.; extensively annotated and commented on ever since.

Tevye der Milchige: Tevye the Dairyman is the main character in the stories of Shalom Aleichem. He has now become the type figure for the ghetto Jews of Eastern Europe.

Torah: The Old Testament of the Bible, which is the foundation of all Jewish law and belief.

Tsar: Title of the emperor and autocrat of all the Russians. The title is derived from the Roman "Caesar," and was held by the Romanov dynasty from 1613 to 1918.

Ukraine: Southern part of the Russian plain. It is now an independent republic. In the past it has been part of Poland, Russia, and Turkey.

Vörwarts: "Forward." The name was used by a large number of different Socialist newspapers. Today the *Forward* is issued weekly in New York in both Yiddish and English.

Walrus: Large members of the seal family whose tusks are used for ivory. Many tusks of dead walrus are washed up each year at the mouth of rivers in Siberia and Alaska.

White Army: All military opponents of the Communist Red Army in the Russian Civil War of 1917–1923.

Yeshiva: Jewish institute of higher learning.

Yiddish: Language derived from medieval German with additions from Hebrew and local languages. For academic purposes it is now divided into Eastern and Western Yiddish. Prior to the turn of the century it was usually considered a dialect or jargon rather than a formal language. It is usually written in Hebrew characters.

Yikkus: Reputation or prestige of Jewish families.

Zaddik: Man of particular holiness whom the Hasidim consider inspired by the Deity and therefore possesses extraordinary wisdom and is capable of giving blessings.

Bibliography

Adler-Rudel, S. *Ostjuden in Deutschland 1880–1940.* Tübingen: J.C.B. Mohr, 1959.

Aleichem, Shalom [Sholem Rabinowitz]. *In the Old Country.* New York: Crown, 1946.

Anonymous. *Hints on Etiquette.* 1836. Reprint. New York: E. P. Dutton, 1951.

Auslandbeauftragter des Senats. *Von Aizenberg bis Zaidelman.* Berlin: Barbara John, May 1995.

Berg, A. Scott. *Goldwyn.* New York: Knopf, 1989.

Bilderarchiv Preussicher Kulturbesitz. *Juden in Preussen.* Dortmund: Hardenberg Kommunikation, 1981.

Birmingham, Steven. *Our Crowd.* New York: Harper & Row, 1967.

Bloomingdale Catalog 1886. Reprint. New York: Dover, 1988.

Bohlman, Philip V. "Musical Life in a Jewish Central European Village." In *Studies in Contemporary Judaism*, Vol. 9, ed. Ezra Mendelsohn. New York: Oxford University Press, 1994.

Brown, Gene. *Movie Time*. New York: Macmillan, 1995.

Bubis, Ignatz (with Edith Kohn). *Ich bin ein Deutscher Staatsbur-ger Jüdischen Glaubens*. Cologne: Kiepenheuer und Witsch, 1993.

Buettner, Wolfgang. *Weberaufstand im Eulengebirge 1844*. Berlin: Deutscher Verlag der Wissenschafler DDR, 1982.

Campbell, Helen. *Darkness and Daylight*. Hartford: A.D. Worthington, 1891.

Cohen, Israel. *Vilna*. Philadelphia: Jewish Publication Society, 1943.

Cohn, Michael. *From Germany to Washington Heights*. New York: Yeshiva University Museum, 1987.

————. *Medieval Justice: The Trial of the Jews of Trent*. New York: Yeshiva University Museum, 1989.

————. *The Jews in Germany, 1945–1993*. Westport, Conn.: Praeger, 1994.

Ellenson, David. "A Disputed Precedent: The Prague Organ in Nineteenth-Century European Legal Literature and Polemics." In *Leo Baeck Institute Yearbook*, Vol. 40. London: Secker & Warburg, 1995.

Englander, David, ed. *Documentary History of the Jewish Immigrants in Britain 1840–1920*. London: Leicester University Press, 1944.

Everett, Susanne. *Lost Berlin*. New York: Bison Books, 1979.

Foner, Philip S. *The Fur and Leather Workers Union*. Newark: Nordan Press, 1950.

Fuchs, Konrad. "Jüdisches Unternehmen in Schlesien. In *Menorah*, eds. Julius H. Schoeps, Karl E. Groeinger, Ludger Heid, and Gerd Mattenhloft. Munich: R. Piper, 1994.

Fuller, J.F.C. *A Military History of the Western World*. New York: Funk & Wagnalls, 1954.

Gabler, Neal. *An Empire of Their Own*. New York: Doubleday, 1989.

Geisel, Eike. *Im Scheunenviertel*. Berlin: Severin and Siebert, 1981.

Gesellschaft für christlich-jüdischer Zusammenarbeit, Dresden. *Juden in Sachsen*. Leipzig: Evangelische Verlagsanstalt, 1994.

Gilbert, Martin. *The Atlas of Jewish History*. New York: Morrow, 1993.

Gitelman, Zvi. *A Century of Ambivalence: The Jews of Russia and the Soviet Union 1881 to the Present*. New York: YIVO Institute for Jewish Research, 1988.

Godey, L. A. *Ladies' Book*. New York: Godey, 1859.

Guggenheim Museum. *Marc Chagall and the Jewish Theater*. New York: Guggenheim Museum, 1992.

Harnick, Sheldon. "If I Were a Rich Man." In *Fiddler on the Roof*, by Joseph Stein based on stories by Sholem Aleichem. RCA Victor Recording LOC 1093.

Hirschler, Gertrude, ed. *Ashkenaz*. New York: Yeshiva University Museum, 1988.

Howe, Irving. *World of Our Fathers*. New York: Simon & Schuster, 1983.

Hurok, Sol (with Ruth Goode). *Impresario, a Memoir*. New York: Random House, 1946.

Idelsohn, A. Z. *Jewish Music*. New York: Schocken Books, 1967.

Kaplan, Marion A. *Die Jüdische Frauenbewegung in Deutschland*. Hamburg: Hans Christians Verlag, 1981.

Karas, Joza. *Music in Terezin*. Stuyvesant, N.Y.: Pendragon Press, 1985.

Kipling, Rudyard. "Rhyme of the Three Sealers." In *Rudyard Kipling's Verse 1885–1918*. New York: Doubleday Co., 1920.

Klee, Ernst, Willy Dressen, and Volker Riess. *Those Were the Days*. Trans. Deborah Burnstone. London: Hamish Hamilton, 1988.

Kybalova, Ludmilla, Olga Herbenova, and Milena Lamarova. *Pictorial Encyclopedia of Fashion*. London: Hamlyn Publications, 1968.

Landsdell, Henry. "Bokhara Revisited." *Scribner's Magazine*, January 1892.

Leipziger Messeamt. *Georg Emanuel Opiz, Ein Zeichner der Leipziger Messe.* Leipzig: 1988.

Lenin, I. V. "The Attitude of the Worker's Party toward Religion." *Proleterii* No. 45, May 1909. Reprint. *Little Lenin Library*, Vol. 7. Bristol, England: n.d.

Leon, Abram. *The Jewish Question, a Marxist Interpretation.* New York: Pathfinder, 1970.

London, Jack. *The Sea Wolf.* New York: Tor, 1995.

Luxemburg, Rosa. *Gesammelte Werke.* 6 volumes. Inst. für Marxismus-Leninismus des Zentralkommittee der SED. Berlin: Dietz, 1974–1979.

Lyon, James K. *Berthold Brecht in America.* London: Methuen, 1982.

Mahler, Raphael. *Hasidism and Jewish Enlightenment.* Trans. Part 1 from Yiddish, Part 2 from Hebrew. Philadelphia: Jewish Publication Society, 1985.

Markgraf, Richard. "Geschichte der Juden auf den Messen von Leipzig 1664–1839." Ph.D. dissertation, Faculty der Philosophie, Universität von Rostock, Bischofswerde, 1894.

Marquand, John P. *Melville Goodwin USA.* Boston: Little, Brown, 1951.

Mayhew, Henry. *London Labor and London Poor.* Edited by Peter Quennell in one volume. London: Spring Books, n.d.

Mendelsohn, Ezra. "On the Jewish Presence in Nineteenth-Century European Musical Life." In *Studies of Contemporary Judaism*, Vol. 9, ed. Ezra Mendelsohn. New York: Oxford University Press, 1994.

Metscher, Klaus, and Walter Fellmann. *Lipsia und Merkur.* Leipzig: Brockhaus Verlag, 1990.

Niewyk, Donald L. *The Jews in Weimar Germany.* Baton Rouge: Louisiana State University Press, 1980.

Osborne, John W. *The Silent Revolution.* New York: Scribner's, 1970.

Pares, Bernard. *A History of Russia.* New York: Knopf, 1928.

Pincus, Max. "Aufstieg der Firma S. Fraenkel, 1827–1900." Ms. in Leo Baeck Institute, New York.

Pipes, Richard. *Russia under the Bolshevik Regime 1919–1924.* New York: Knopf, 1994.

Plaskin, Glenn. *Horowitz.* New York: Morrow, 1983.

Rastorgueva, Ludmilla. *Clothes of the North, National Dress of the Sakha Republic.* Yarkutsk, Russia, 1994.

Reinharz, Jehuda. *Chaim Weizmann, The Making of a Zionist Leader.* New York: Oxford University Press, 1985.

Riis, Jacob A. "Children of the Poor." *Scribner's Magazine,* May 1892.

Ringelblum, Emmanuel. *Notes from the Warsaw Ghetto.* New York: Schocken Books, 1974.

Rosenfeld, Morris. *Lieder des Ghettos.* Trans. Berthold Feiwel. Berlin: Herrman Seeman, 1902.

Roth, Cecil, ed. *The Standard Jewish Encyclopedia.* Garden City, N.Y.: Doubleday, 1959.

Rubinstein, Arthur. *My Young Years.* New York: Knopf, 1973.

Runciman, Steven. *History of the Crusades.* Cambridge: Cambridge University Press, 1951.

Rurup, Reinhard, ed. *Topographie des Terrors.* Berlin: Willmuth Arenhovel, 1988.

"Russia, Russia, Russia." *Fortune Magazine,* March 1932.

Salamander, Rachel, ed. *Jewish World of Yesterday 1860–1938.* Trans. Eileen Walliser-Schwarzbart. New York: Rizzoli, 1991.

Sanders, Ronald. *The Downtown Jews.* New York: Harper & Row, 1969. Reprint. New York: Dover, 1987.

Scheiger, Brigitte. "Juden in Berlin." In *Zuwanderern zu Einheimischen,* ed. Stefi Jersch-Wenzel and Barbara John. Berlin: Nicolai, 1990.

Schildhauer, Johannes. *The Hansa.* Trans. Katehrine Vanovitch. Leipzig: Dorse Press, 1988.

Schramil, Rudolf. *Stadtverfassung nach Magdeburger Recht*, ed. Dr. Otto Gierke. Breslau: Untersuchungen der Staats und Rechtsgeschichte, Heft 125, 1915.

Sears Roebuck Catalogue 1897. Reprint. New York: Chelsea House Publishers, 1968.

Semyonov, Yuri. *The Conquest of Siberia.* Trans. E. W. Dickes. London: Routledge & Sons, 1944.

Shmeruk, Chrone. "The Purimspil." In *Purim: The Face and the Mask.* New York: Yeshiva University Museum, 1979.

Spargo, John. *The Bitter Cry of Children.* New York: Grosset & Dunlap, 1906.

Spielberg, D. Steven (director). *Schindler's List.* Video LDMCA 081629.

Thompson, Virgil. *A Virgil Thompson Reader.* Boston: Little, Brown, and Co., 1981.

Troller, Karl. "Leipziger Pelzhandel 1902–1904." Ms. in Leo Baeck Institute, New York.

Trotsky, Leon. *History of the Russian Revolution.* Trans. Max Eastman. New York: Simon & Schuster, 1934.

Unger, Manfred, and Hubert Lang. *Juden in Leipzig, Eine Dokumentation.* Leipzig: 1988.

Waletzky, Josh (director). *Image Before My Eyes.* Video. YIVO Institute for Jewish Research. Distr. by Ergo Media, Teaneck, N.J., 1991.

Weigert, Abraham. "Erinnerung 1895." Ms. in Leo Baeck Institute, New York.

Wertheimer, Jack. *Unwelcome Strangers.* New York: Oxford University Press, 1987.

Westphal, Uwe. *Berliner Konfektion und Mode.* 2nd ed. Berlin: Edition Hentrich, 1988.

Wolberger, Lionel. "Music in Holy Argument." In *Studies in Contemporary Judaism*, Vol. 9, ed. Ezra Mendelsohn. New York: Oxford University Press, 1994.

Zborowski, Mark, and Elizabeth Herzog. *Life Is with People.* New York: International University Press, 1952.

Index

About the Author

MICHAEL COHN is Adjunct Anthropologist at the Yeshiva University Museum in New York City and a guest lecturer at the University of Leipzig and Schiller University, Jena, Germany. He has spent twenty-five years teaching at the Brooklyn Children's Museum. His other publications include *Jews in Germany 1945–1993* (Praeger, 1994).